'Ed Cowan sets out full of hope, suffers numerous setbacks, curses himself, blames his diary, sympathises with his wife, tries growing vegetables, tinkers with his game, seeks to master his mind, plays some inspired innings, almost subdues the Poms and eventually triumphs in the Sheffield Shield final. This is the story of a single cricketer and every cricketer. It is the tale of one season and every season.' – **Peter Roebuck**

'This is the real deal: the highs, lows, joys and toils of a professional cricketer described with refreshing honesty and intelligence. If you've ever wondered what it takes to achieve success, handle failure, cope with pressure and deal with doubt while playing with Australia's best cricketers, Ed Cowan can tell you.' – **Gideon Haigh**

IN THE FIRING LINE

ED COWAN plays for the PKF Tasmanian Tigers. He grew up in Sydney and enjoyed five seasons with the NSW Speedblitz Blues before taking up an offer from the Tasmanian Tigers, hoping to re-ignite his career. Cowan ended up the second-highest Sheffield Shield run scorer in 2009–2010 – his 957 runs included a double century and two centuries. He has played cricket around the world and, in winter 2010, he scored a century for Australia A against Sri Lanka A in a convincing series win. He lives in Hobart with his wife Virginia.

IN THE
FIRING
LINE *Diary of a Season*

ED COWAN

NEWSOUTH

A NewSouth book
Published by
NewSouth Publishing
University of New South Wales Press Ltd
University of New South Wales
Sydney NSW 2052
AUSTRALIA
newsouthpublishing.com

© Ed Cowan 2011
First published 2011
10 9 8 7 6 5 4 3 2 1

National Library of Australia Cataloguing-in-Publication entry
     Author: Cowan, Ed., 1982–
     Title: In the firing line: diary of a season/Ed Cowan.
     ISBN: 978 174223 315 4 (pbk.)
     ISBN: 978 174224 102 9 (ebook: epub)
     Subjects: Cowan, Ed., 1982–
          Cricket players – Tasmania – Anecdotes.
          Cricket – Tasmania.
          Cricket – Tasmania – Anecdotes.
     Dewey Number: 796.35826092

Design Xou Creative
Cover photographs Rick Smith, David Bellamy
Printer Ligare

Contents

Foreword

If you follow Australian cricket reasonably closely, you know the name Ed Cowan. If you follow cricket but less closely, you may not have. If you check in on the game occasionally, as in catching it on the television news, or occasionally listening to the ABC, he'll almost certainly be a stranger to you. Chances are that even if you do try to keep up with the game, you have probably not seen him bat. That's okay. It's just the way it is.

Ed is 29. He's been playing first-class cricket for eight years. In 2009, he left his native New South Wales for Tasmania, for whom he's enjoyed two very good seasons, and been picked for Australia A. In 2009–10 he was the top scorer in the home and away rounds of the Sheffield Shield; in 2010–11, he was Man of the Match in the Sheffield Shield final.

That still leaves Ed excluded from the tightly focused and dazzling limelight inhabited by the elite of the elite in the Australian team – he is, so far, a nearly man. Yet 'nearly' in Australian cricket is a world as high-pressure as it is low-key. It is a world tantalisingly close to fame while still mired in obscurity; it is a world Ed brings to life in this perceptive, candid, brave and illuminating diary of his 2010–11 season.

I'm biased. I know Ed. We met some years ago when fortuitously on the same side in a charity match at the Sydney Cricket Ground. The character of this game can be judged from the fact that with the scores tied off the final ball, Mick Molloy bowled me an underarm. Ed was rather more serious. He had many theories on the game, of rather greater sophistication than the importance of getting it in the right areas generally in proximity to the corridor of uncertainty. Being likewise inclined, we got to talking, and stayed in touch.

Good thinkers don't always write well, but they have a head start. When Ed expressed an appreciation of some player diaries he had read, I wondered aloud why he didn't do his own, and offered to help if he did. Why? Not only because he was capable of it, but because I recognised him as an honest man, carried away neither by self-importance nor sportsman's ego. Ed *does* have an ego: an appealing low-level self-belief that chivvies him along in his pursuit of higher standards. But he has no tickets on himself, no image to protect, or huge fanbase to satisfy. I thought he could tell me what cricket is *really* like. And I believe he has.

Cricket is a slippery, tricky, testing game for its practitioners. You can be in the form of your life, nick one early and spend the rest of the day smouldering. You can feel like you're defending a barn door with a broomstick, yet somehow come out the other side and make hay. In the course of a season, there are days you feel sorry for the people who don't play cricket and know its satisfactions. There are days you wish you'd never heard of it, when you depend on your mates and your memories to carry you along.

Frankly, too, you encounter variations on these themes at all levels of the game. Last summer, I was yarning after a day's play to a Yarras teammate – a good cricketer who had given the game away for a while, made a successful comeback with us then hit a lean trot before that afternoon making a good score. In everyday club life, he is the proverbial son of fun, always with a quip on his lips, or the administering of an atomic wedgie on his mind. He surprised me by coming straight out and saying that the runs had come in the nick of time; he'd been losing sleep over not contributing to the team, and wondering why he was putting himself through something he was not enjoying. 'Welcome to my world', I said lightly; but we both knew what he meant.

For the first-class cricketer, it's an even greater challenge. When game time comes around, he can't just say he'd rather play golf or find a beach somewhere. Cricket is his job, and as a job obliges him to put things right, to deal with the constant natural undulations of form, fortune and opportunity as best he can. Enjoyment still plays a part: domestic cricketers are not paid enough for it to be otherwise. But what counts is the ability to preserve that vital spark of confidence and commitment when it gutters in the draught of failure. You'll cheer for Ed during his moments of individual success in this book, perhaps the more so for knowing about his interludes of hair-yanking frustration and brooding self-laceration.

The other invaluable feature of Ed's diary is the insight it affords into the state of cricket in Australia, much debated and theorised on last summer, and the subject of a much-heralded report commissioned by Cricket Australia. Those who play the game best in Australia are seldom solicited for their views about the game, as distinct from their own games within it. There's the annual poll by the Australian Cricketers' Association revealing that 124 per cent of respondents would like more money; otherwise you're left to guess what guys are thinking by reading between the tweets.

Ed has views. He puts them fearlessly and well. He loves cricket – he also has a degree in finance, and interest in the wider world, which helps him put the game in perspective. He has the kind of informed and reasoned slant on affairs that this country, with its administration in a mess and its Test match ranking in free fall, could do with much more of. This, then, is not just a thoughtful and eye-opening book but a necessary one in a voice both fresh and frank. You'll like Ed. I do.

Gideon Haigh

Acknowledgments

It could be well argued that watching someone write is not a very pleasurable past-time. My poor wife Virginia had to endure this day after day during the past season. She not only embraced her 'cricket-widow' stature with compassion and support, but somehow managed to put up with my mental absence long after the day's play had finished and the night's writing had begun. She also skilfully helped type up and edit my handwritten scribble, when the season had finally finished and my motivation to complete the next stage of the diary was waning.

I owe a huge public thank you to Gideon for not only writing the foreword, but also having a little blind faith in the project from the start. His direction and confidence gave me great strength to be brave and honest. Before the manuscript had hit the publisher's desk, his diligent and critical eye had already spent innumerable hours guiding and editing. Without him too, I doubt the diary would exist in its current form.

To the players and coaching staff at the Tasmanian Tigers, thank you for making these past two years the most enjoyable of my career. We all have a special bond that should be cherished. Thank you for letting me document our collective experiences. This diary is not only my story, but the story of our entire team. We now have a record of a remarkably special season. More than anyone, I hope you guys enjoy reading this book.

Introduction

I have always been a 'jotter' of things. To-do lists can be found on endless pieces of paper throughout the house. Cricket has fallen in with that habit. Since 2002 I have kept a cricket diary – not a journal of daily events but a 'batting bible' with thoughts on the game, opponents, motivational philosophies, records of performances. So much is the diary part of my preparatory rites that I feel flustered if I can't see it sitting in my cricket bag while I am padding up.

Other cricketers have always regarded the habit as a little odd. When he was playing for my club in Sydney, Kevin Pietersen scribbled 'keep it fucking interesting' on the inside cover. We're all different, and for me it has worked. Once I've committed myself to print of an evening, my head feels uncluttered and my thoughts simple.

The idea of keeping a full-scale diary of a season came gradually. A catalyst was reading Ed Smith's diary of a season playing for Kent, *On and Off the Field*. I felt as though he had put on paper all the thoughts on cricket I had ever had, albeit somewhat more eloquently. I started copying large passages into a note pad. I admired his candour. Although cricket is a team sport, players rarely give much away about their inner-most thoughts. In an environment so fierce and competitive, it is taboo to show doubt. Smith's book gave me courage to confront mine.

Another huge catalyst was crossing paths and since becoming friends with Gideon Haigh. Ever since I was young, one of his books has been given to me as a Christmas present. Reading his work had taught me that there is more to the game than the scorecard. In discussing Ed Smith's book, he mentioned that I should consider something similar. It made me see the story in our story – that is, the story of we domestic cricketers. The interstate and the international games are far apart. Participants are scraping to make a living. Below us is the long drop back to the amateurism of club cricket. On any given day each of the six states could beat each other in any format of the game. Everyone is competing on an individual basis for higher honours, while trying to maintain a supportive team environment.

Perhaps the best description of our plight came from a friend far more artistically inclined than me. He suggested that the best way to think about domestic cricketers is similar to that of Off Broadway actors. We're in a production we sincerely wish to succeed in but which we acknowledge few people will ever see; we're hoping also, from a personal standpoint, that there'll be a big director or talent scout in the audience who'll identify sufficient promise in us that we'll graduate to a bigger stage. Who knows, of course, when they'll be watching, what they'll notice, or even whether they'll have room for us? Who can tell what sort of production we'll be cast in, the kind of run we'll get, the kind of response from the critics? That's where luck comes in as well as skill. But it's what we have, and everyone is in the same position.

It was over Easter in 2009 that I decided to leave my home state of NSW and accept a two-year contract to play for Tasmania. After five seasons in and out of the NSW team, disrupted by two major injuries, I felt as though I was not improving as I wished to, not enjoying my cricket as I desired, and not getting the opportunities I deserved (rightly or wrongly). I felt I had done my apprenticeship. I wanted to excel.

I immediately fell in love with Tasmania. Led by George Bailey, and heavily influenced by former captain Dan Marsh and the current coaching staff, the culture was progressive and inclusive. I felt like a new person with nothing to lose, free of any previous preconception, and more decisive generally – I also married my girlfriend, who had loyally and self-sacrificingly come with me. My off-field happiness, coupled with a clear head, a defined role to open the batting and a huge amount of hard work led to my most successful season as a professional cricketer. Tasmania won the one-day domestic competition; I scored more runs than any other player in the competition during the regular rounds of the Sheffield Shield; I was the state's Shield Cricketer of the Year.

The decision I made to keep a diary of my second season in Tasmania was a mark of the confidence I felt approaching 2010–11. Setting myself the maintenance of it as a challenge seemed like another bold decision – I was giving myself something to live up to, by saying inwardly that there would be achievements worth recording. I felt like I was ready for anything. I also knew that cricket is a fickle game.

For those not familiar with either the PKF Tasmanian Tigers or the structure of the Australian domestic season, a short reference section with brief descriptions of both can be found at the back of the book.

Diary of a season

Monday, 4 October 2010

There is still snow on the top of Mount Wellington, and icy winds have been sniping about the nets at Bellerive Oval, from which goalposts have only just been removed – cricket season must be around the corner. In fact, it's virtually in the house next door. While grade cricket will not start in Hobart for a couple more weeks (having already been well and truly underway in other states), the PKF Tasmanian Tigers' first game of 2010–11 is only two days away.

Today was essentially the first time the entire squad had been together all pre-season. It was the first time, for example, we had been joined by our new import, Mark Cosgrove from South Australia, who returned yesterday from another successful season with Glamorgan. Cossie is at a crossroad, having been strangely axed by his own state. Privately, we can't believe our luck. He is a player of enormous skill – someone who has benefited from playing cricket all year round and in doing so, learning to play the game his way – cramming 90 first-class games into his 26 years. He's tough. I've crossed swords with him on the field many times over. Everything's different, though, when you share dressing rooms; in fact, having made the hard decision to come to Tasmania last season, I feel a kinship with him. I hope, like me, he can reinvent himself away from the hometown preconceptions.

Not that he is the only one in our group for whom this season holds greater significance. My friend and captain, George Bailey, could well be in contention for a spot in the World Cup squad come February if he continues from where he left off in last year's limited-over competition. His appointment as leader last year went a long way to making my decision to move to Tasmania all the more clear. He was someone I thought I wanted to play under and for. I saw him first as an opponent, and admired his natural gifts and obvious cricket savvy. I got to know him when we represented our respective state playing groups as delegates on the Australian Cricketers' Association, a serious environment in which he also showed his silly side: at an ACA karaoke night, he performed The Archies' 'Sugar Sugar' with several kilograms of CSR's finest granulated product trapped in his undies.

George has grown into his role as captain, as an on-field strategist and off-field motivator. What he needs now is a knockout season with the bat – 1000 runs instead of 700, the kind that lifts him into Test contention. His 160 not out for Australia A in the winter may also be the catalyst for the huge first-class season that his talent deserves.

In a country that has been reportedly bare of a spinner of any substance in the post-Warne era, we are in the sometimes awkward position of having both the next best spinners not playing international cricket in our team, Xavier Doherty and Jason Krejza. Unfortunately, Bellerive Oval has historically given little encouragement to slow bowlers: Stuart MacGill described it once as though he was bowling on glass. But perhaps though if the wicket is grassy this year, the old adage, 'if it seams, it spins', will ring true.

They are brilliant in their own ways: Xavier has the skill to mix up his pace and rarely bowls a bad ball; Jason turns it big, perhaps as much as anyone in the world.

The real complexity of our situation as a team though is how we are meant to fit both of these guys into our four-day team. It is simply not possible, except perhaps in Sydney on a turning wicket. Either could play Test cricket this year, and yet only one will ever be playing regular four-day cricket. It is not an enviable position – whoever is playing is doing so with the other one looming over his shoulder. Xavier is the incumbent, having stormed back into the side last year following four seasons of being typecast as a one-day player. He finished the season as the player voted 'Player of the Year'. This would have no doubt been a dose of tough reality for Jason, who fewer than two seasons earlier took 12 wickets in his Test debut. He probably feels hard done by, but I do think the constant competition has brought the best out in each.

I've avoided the Hobart winter by playing club cricket in the quirky cricket community of the Netherlands. It was an absolutely fantastic cricket and life experience, broken up nicely by some serious cricket for the Australian A series against Sri Lanka. I feel mentally fresh and re-energised, but still aware of the need to lift my mental sharpness – being back in a professional environment will help.

As is often the way for Tassie, our first game of the year is in Brisbane at The Gabba. In the past, it has served up vividly green pitches full of pace and bounce. I've known Sheffield Shield games where it's been impossible to distinguish the wicket from the square until the groundsman started up his roller. Three days have generally been long enough for a result.

Our first game, however, is under the new one-day playing conditions – a 45-over, split-innings game – the brainchild of Cricket Australia, an attempt to revive the one-day game following the challenge posed by T20. Playing condition changes include all 12 players taking part in the game (11 on the field), two five-over power plays (1–5 and 20–25; the opening five overs of the second innings), a maximum of four fielders outside the ring, a maximum of 12 overs per bowler, greater flexibility on leg-side wide adjudication and the allowance of a second bouncer per over (a fantastic addition!). Radical indeed. It disappoints me somewhat that CA did not tinker more with a single-innings game prior to discarding it altogether.

But we've cleared our heads of any initial misgivings and planned how we are going to retain our title as the premier one-day team in the country. We think the key, match-winning contests of the game are the initial first five-over power play, the five overs leading into the first break and the first five overs after it (also a power play).

For us, long gone are assigned batting orders. Rather,

everything is dictated by the situation and flow of the game. We don't want our nurdlers (Cowan) having to force the issue in power plays; nor do we want to expose the hitters (Bailey and Birt) to a swinging new ball (two used) if we lose early wickets. The batsmen have spoken of the need to be able to play controlled, aggressive and instinctive pull-shots to ensure both bouncers are not automatic 'bankable' dot balls, and also the need to develop our sweeping simply to exploit field restrictions. The bowlers have accented early wickets and containing into the break with effective bouncers and the use of our spinners. Fielding, of course, is key. Last year, as champions, we had the highest effected run-out percentage – not to say we didn't give away our fair share of chances either, with Cowan and Bailey impersonating the 90s Pakistani middle order on several occasions. We also had the highest percentage of successful catch attempts. As a group we have huge confidence in our one-day game stemming from winning three competitions of the last five, and feel that the playing condition changes really suit our style of play and team balance. We will certainly take some beating – my early prediction is that we will be there at season's end holding up another one-day trophy.

Tuesday, 5 October

Despite the obviousness of the situation, it was not until I had finished the familiar summer act of packing my kit bag that it dawned on me that the season is really about to start. As a kid, it used to be such a simple thing to do – I could have my bag packed and unpacked in a matter of seconds. Now it is an involved, prolonged, painstaking process. By the time you have packed both sets of pads (white and coloured), multiple gloves and bats and assorted paraphernalia, as well as three full sets of whites and colours, jumpers, socks and the rest of the required training uniform, there seems to be very little room for a decent shirt, casual shoes and a clean pair of undies. This particular trip required two full-sized cricket bags. At least packing is a happy experience at this end of the tour – you are still filled with hope and expectation. Any cricketer will tell you, there is nothing worse than packing your cricket bag after losing (particularly when you have a habit of spreading everything across the change room, like me).

I am rooming with one of our all-rounders, Luke Butterworth, this trip. His laid-back approach to the world makes for an easy week. Not that we have any in this particular team, but I have certainly roomed with some intense characters, who want nothing more but to talk through a ball-by-ball description of their innings and eventual dismissal long after the event. That can make your hotel downtime more exhausting than the fixture itself. We pair a batter and a bowler these days, which seems to help the harmony. The days of 'sharing a room', and waking to find your companion shadow-batting in the nude, are past – we are very lucky to be housed in superb two-bedroom serviced apartments. Touring isn't what it used to be ...

Like middle-distance runners or heavyweight boxers, the day before a game is about getting the mind in a performance headspace, and certainly varies from player to player. I like to be sharp for 20 balls in the nets and then 'top-up' a specific skill in a throw-down net with a coach. For me, gone are the days of a huge volume of hitting balls the day before. Cricket is a contest played in the middle: overtraining can actually make you flat if your game is in running order. Busy cricketers constantly tread this line. It gets to a point where you need to take a step back and relax – nothing will change technically one day to the next.

I've been working hard for almost nine months on my dynamic batting – hitting the ball hard and over-the-top, giving me the ability to clear the rope on demand. It is something that certainly does not come naturally. Playing in a strong team like NSW can make you selfish: because you constantly felt on trial, you tended to leave the risks to others. The Tigers coaching staff, however, are constantly looking for ways you can improve: they identified this as a means by which I could broaden my contribution to the team by filling different positions in the batting order. I haven't come as far as I would have liked just yet. Learning to 'hit' (so to speak) from scratch meant dealing with the emotions of initial inadequacy. Although onlookers would hardly have noticed, an innings of 60 off fewer balls in the Ford Ranger Cup Final felt to me like a breakthrough.

Following on from this, one of my goals for the coming one-day season is to have a strike-rate of 80 or better if batting in the top three. Historically I am in the high 60s – embarrassing. It is nice to have a few new tricks that the opposition are not expecting. Generally, regardless of when I bat, I want to be positive. Too often last year my first resort was running the ball to third man, not only for a maximum of one run, but a lot of the time, hitting it straight to backward point. This summer, I want to loosen up and be positive. Yes, I will be trying hard to relax. Batting – it's full of paradoxes.

I don't tend to have any fixed 'night before' rituals. It seems they emerge as the season progresses. As though a new season brings a clean slate of order and routines that slowly bubble to the surface once some success has been had. The security blanket of, 'I had a bowl of pasta and a glass of red before my last hundred' seems strange writing about, but certainly happens subconsciously. A lean season with the bat is at least compensated to some degree by a wide variety of touring cuisine!

Wednesday, 6 October
Tasmania 9–252 defeated Queensland 247 all out

Thursday, 7 October (pm)
Day/night fixtures can really mess around with your body clock. Often you don't arrive back to the hotel until after 11 pm, having to go through various recovery treatments after the last ball is bowled. Worse still, the mind is flying; buzzing with emotion and adrenaline usually until the early hours of the morning.

The game itself turned out to be a bottler. Dead and buried, needing 67 off 32 balls with just a solitary wicket in hand, Queensland's number 11, Nathan Rimmington, went berserk. On a wicket that all batsmen had struggled to get in on, Rimmington pounded 42 off 24 to reduce the requirement to 41 off 18, 29 off 12, then 17 off the last over. When the first ball went for four, it is fair to say some panic, if it had not already, set in among the Tassie boys on the field. Finally, 6 were needed off the last delivery. Brendan Drew, who had bowled beautifully all night, bowled a waist-high full toss wide of off. It should have disappeared; Rimmington dragged it on. Often when the impossible becomes feasible, tail-enders fail to deliver. With something to lose, the body tenses up, and the mind clouds. He had played one hell of a cameo – if it had come off, it would no doubt have gone down in Queensland cricket folklore.

Prior to the grandstand finish, Mark Cosgrove in his first game for Tasmania despatched the new ball to all corners with a run-a-ball 65. I failed. I felt relaxed and in control – perhaps too relaxed on a wicket with some assistance from bowlers – and nicked a decent length ball that nipped across me, having pitched in line with the stumps. Disappointed and frustrated, I have replayed it over several times in my mind. Decent ball, yes – but I always feel as though good players, one of which I'm aspiring to be, should keep them out. Had it been a four-day game, I'd have let it go. I now have to do the same to that thought – let it go. Negativity around failure can be debilitating – the contest is over, we won, I felt like I was in the moment and was pleased I contributed in the field to make up for my lack of runs.

Tomorrow, the Sheffield Shield season begins. Continually

changing in and out of formats for one game at a time takes significant mental skill. While I'm sure the pressures of international cricket are huge, this is one issue that they never have to deal with.

Friday, 8 October

Tasmania 1–33 vs Queensland

Play started at 2.15 pm and only lasted an hour – rain ruining the opening day of the Australian first-class season. It could have been a lot worse. In dark, drizzly conditions, on a green grassy wicket, Bails called incorrectly and Queensland took a nano-second to decide that they would bowl.

As the coin hung in the air, I quietly prayed we would win the toss, and I could stave off batting. In such situations, you put on a brave face, and pretend you're happy to play regardless – but you are lying. Pure negativity. No one says it, but everyone is thinking it.

The funny thing is that when Bails signalled we were batting, I immediately felt good and resolved. I started to think about the challenge. The Gabba can become a minefield if you let it. I planned to bat a long way out of my crease, and a long way across my stumps – allowing me to leave on length confidently and also to try to get the bowlers to bowl straight at me so I could play the ball under my eyes. It would take some skill to execute, but it made sense to me. Often, even if your plan is flawed, just having one gives you clarity and purpose.

On my way out, I jokingly asked the physio to say a quick

prayer to St Christopher for a slice or two of luck – often needed in any innings, let alone in the conditions that were about to greet me. By this time, however, I had talked myself into a state of excitement. This is why I play the game. I focused on each ball as a personal contest. Such was the bubble of competition I had created, I had not realised it had been raining steadily for a good seven or eight overs when play was stopped and eventually called off for the day. I hope that intensity can return in the morning. Runs on these kinds of wickets need to be fought for, but are treasured and remembered – more so by teammates than spectators of the game.

Saturday, 9 October

No play due to rain.

Boredom, anticipation and frustration can only describe my day. I am so mentally exhausted from thinking 'stay up and focused, you could be out there at any moment', that I don't have the energy to write. My book and bed wait for me.

Sunday, 10 October

Tasmania 2–52 vs Queensland (only 11 overs played)

This has started to get ridiculous. To add to the frustration of the situation, 48 hours after facing the last ball of the 17th over, play resumed for just 50 minutes at 4.45 pm, under lights and in light drizzle. Having survived the first six overs in good shape, I misjudged an outswinger, having set up for Rimmington's stock inswinger, and nicked a straight 'push' as the ball zipped across me: I need to remind myself to stay side on, even if opening up to access the ball and lead with my front shoulder. I made 19 in what was essentially 50 participating and mentally active hours: I need to appreciate the absurdity of that too. There is no game on the planet that can justify such ridiculousness.

There is no escaping that awful feeling of failure that engulfs you when you are dismissed. The obligatory self-cursing is followed by a mental replay of the dismissal as you saw it. Almost a kind of self-therapy, you try to justify to yourself what on earth just happened. All this can take place even before stepping a foot in the change room. Today it was a lingering analysis. I sat with a towel over my head, angry, not wanting to face the outside world, urging myself to get on with the impending reality of grabbing a drink and calming down. Why was I so angry given that the game is essentially dead? The forecast tomorrow is for flooding rain. The answer is that I just hate getting out – hate giving any satisfaction to the bowler – hate knowing that on this occasion he was better than me. I was also angry at myself for having tinkered with my preparation. For my legs were heavy. With no prospect of play at 11 am, we had all headed to the gym to avoid the cabin fever of the previous day that is associated with the hibernation of a rainy dressing room. I was wary of the prospect of batting later in the day, but still pumped out a solid session. Looking back, that 5 per cent physical sharpness lost at the gym may have cost me my wicket.

Regardless of conditions, I expect to score runs, and runs are what you get judged by. Sometimes, though, how many runs you make is not an actual index of how 'well' you are batting – luck plays such a huge part in our fortunes. The cricketer's job in 'managing' his game and mental state, then, is to control this disappointment when the runs and feelings are mismatched, in the belief that in the long run they will eventually be more closely aligned.

Despite all of this, patches of failure normally leave you in an empty state of doubt. After all, we are only ever competing against ourselves – our own discipline, patience and preparation – yet this is overlooked by the fact that your contribution to the team is entirely objective.

When people talk about 'experience' or 'level headedness', I think they are actually describing how you deal with failure and your response to disappointment. It takes some time, and I do think I am over the hump in learning this skill. In a great season, you may only have five or six great days – between times, a streak of masochism is handy.

Monday, 11 October
Match abandoned at 11.30 am

The match was drawn. For us, it almost constituted a defeat. Generally speaking, you count on The Gabba to produce an outright result and 6 points. In a competition that is so closely contested, where 6 points can separate second and the right to compete in the final from last, giving away such an opportunity to win such valuable points is disheartening.

This is compounded by the fact that our home wicket is historically very placid. Other states like Queensland and

WA have the luxury of knowing that their home games tend to produce results; we don't.

Only two of five games at Bellerive last year ended in results – one of which was a set-up run chase of 350 off 85 overs. It was a game that I will remember for the rest of my career and beyond; Tasmania were 9 down, needing 10 off the last over, with the experienced Ashley Noffke bowling to our young keeper Brady Jones, in his second game, with our resident bunny Tim MacDonald as his partner. The first ball resulted in a single that left MacDonald on strike. He promptly hit it straight to cover and ran, but the fielder panicked, and gave away an overthrow attempting a direct hit. With 8 required off two balls, Jones somehow reverse lapped Noffke to third man, where Brett Dorey looked to be chasing it down only to collapse as though he'd been picked off by a sniper, his achilles tendon having snapped. The ball trickled into the fence as he lay helplessly watching. After a five-minute delay as he was stretchered from the ground, Jones backed away and sliced a yorker through backward point for another boundary to win the match.

Writing about that particular game has brought shivers to my spine. If it had been televised, it would have been talked about by the masses for months. As it were, the 'incredible' in domestic cricket was confined to a few paragraphs in the back section of the sports pages and would have been forgotten by those not present before they had finished their morning coffee – sometimes it really does feel like we are invisible cricketers.

Tuesday, 12 October

One of the few downsides of living in Hobart is the fact that for us to get to or from most cities, we have to catch two flights, and going home after a long week away can take up an entire day – depending on connecting flight times into a poorly serviced Hobart airport. It does not sound like much of an issue, but when the turnaround is only two days, as it is this week with a one-day game in Adelaide, it means six flights in a week. On the upside it gives me some guaranteed personal time to catch up on diary writing and collect my thoughts.

Wednesday, 13 October

Even with only two days at home, of which neither was a designated rest day, I felt like I needed a bit of a fine-tuning session with our batting coach Michael Di Venuto (Diva). Diva has over 300 games of first-class cricket under his belt, and his eye and feel for batting are second to none. Good coaches don't have to have been good players themselves, but I know the two coaches who I have clicked with the most over the years, Diva and Graham Thorpe, were both phenomenal players in their prime. Because both were left-handed top-order batsman, I feel as though they have fought the same battles that I have; in fact, I've become a firm believer in left-handed batting coaches for left-handed batters (and vice versa): the worlds of left- and right-handers are like different games covered by the same laws.

Diva (and Thorpey) are both strong technically. One

thing they've stressed is the importance of opening up a little in my stance to access the inswinger. How much? Just enough. Open up too much and you start nicking them; not enough and you kick them in front of the stumps. Batting technique management is like treading a tightrope high above the circus. Both coaches, though, talk mainly about 'how to score runs', particularly when faced with awkward and trying conditions, against a large variety of bowling styles. They make training into a planning session. Inevitably the mid-session conversations have deep technical elements, but they are based around adapting your technical skills in differing circumstances and developing the confidence to adjust accordingly, often mid-game if required.

I worked hard today on keeping my shape in my shots while not giving away access to the ball – staying side on, but not closing off so that I limited my shots down the ground. I regained that feeling of my momentum and weight transfer, the rhythm that feels natural but you have to paradoxically work to find – a kind of flow from a solid base where you are hitting the ball late and with minimum effort, which sometimes you can lose through trying to hit too hard. Despite being mentally fatigued from a week away, any session with Diva is worth it and today was no exception.

Saturday, 16 October

We spent today preparing for our one-day game against SA tomorrow. The Adelaide Oval has always held a large soft spot in my heart. I grew up listening to my grandfather telling me stories of watching Bradman play here in his pomp. When I made my first-class debut here six seasons ago, the fixtures and fittings of the change rooms were originals from the era of Bodyline – the huge showerheads obviously long pre-dated thoughts of drought. The glimpse of the cathedral beyond the old scoreboard seemed to transport you back in time. Despite the completion of a new western grandstand, I was pleased to find the aura of the ground undiminished, the façade of the famous arches having been incorporated in the new mega structure.

Despite it being 13 degrees and damp, the rain cleared long enough for not only a fielding session, but also a turf net session. Being the day before a game and eager for runs having missed out last week, I felt in need of a solid hit. My rhythms against bowlers had been thrown out by two weeks of constant rain and I was determined that today was going to be the day I would find them again. Or so I thought. My first three balls seamed and popped off a length on the soft wickets. It is amazing how defensive something so simple can make you feel. My footwork became anchored to the crease, my hands started reaching out in front of my body, and my bat felt like a miscellaneous and heavy piece of wood.

Thankfully Ali DeWinter, our assistant coach, cooled me down with ten gentle throw-downs: 'Just watch, make a step and hit it', he said, as though he was babysitting a nine-year-old. 'Get out', he said after the tenth. 'You're ready.' I was ready; I just didn't know it at the time. I sat down, did some shadow batting like a kid impersonating one of his favourite players in the backyard, and kept repeating to myself, 'Get forward, be aggressive, bang it back past him'. Only now, several hours later, have I calmed completely.

After training, I took a long solo drive out to Hamley Bridge to see my grandmother. It was a good reality check. I hadn't visited her farm since my grandfather's funeral eight years ago. We sat and chatted about making marmalade, the secret to baking the perfect scones, and also shed a few tears over my mother's ill health. We walked around the garden talking about why her tomatoes taste so good – incredible given she is 92 this year – and I changed some light bulbs – an everyday act that felt a special gift. It was an emotional couple of hours. There is a chance this was to be my last trip out to her property. It may well be the last time I see her.

As professional cricketers, we play a game that is never a matter of life or death – and here I was, stressed about a bloody net session. Feeling good the day before a game can give you a false sense of security – you can forget to work hard when you get your chance in the middle. But I am going to enjoy tomorrow, and regardless of results, play with a huge infectious smile.

Sunday, 17 October

Tasmania 6–274 (Cowan 75, Cosgrove 61, Bailey 50)
defeated SA 183 (Doherty 3–20) by 91 runs

Monday, 18 October

I came to the crease yesterday in the ninth over after a sluggish start and settled quickly. I think the Adelaide Oval can have that effect. You don't feel as though you are in the spotlight of a cauldron stadium, but rather playing in the park on a picnic outing. I have tasted success here before – my last two one-day hits in Adelaide have seen runs – and the middle was pleasingly familiar. The wicket, although a little tacky, was a good one, and I knew I had to be aggressive. Early on, Duval over-pitched and I timed a straight-ish leg side clip. Off the bat it felt like two, but it had hit the fence before I had reached the other end. I was away.

In the 18th over, two before the forced innings change, the left arm spinner came on, and despite both straight fielders being out, I played out a maiden. Embarrassing. The first one gripped and spun, the other five, playing for spin, skidded into the bat before I could time it into a gap. With no deep point, the grip of the first ball had suckered me into trying to hit with the spin through the on side.

Retaining the strike for the last over, another dot from the spinner caused a little anxiety. Competing thoughts ran through my head: after six dots, time to take a risk; on the brink of the break, not a time to take a risk. A few years ago I would have heeded the second voice; now I obeyed the first and premeditated a slog sweep. As he ran in, I was muttering: 'Go on, go for it, do it with conviction'. I made a move early across my stumps, and despite the ball being nowhere near where I wanted it to be, I took a mighty swing across the line and connected solidly. It took several seconds (or so it seemed) to pick up the exact location of the ball – a moment of panic: has it gone straight up? But hearing clapping from the dressing room, I turned to see the ball trickle into the short square boundary.

One-day cricket is a constant battle of managing the relationship with the 'evil' risk-taking devil that sits on your shoulder while you bat. He is the one who constantly wants you to try to hit over the top when the game does not demand it, feeding your ego with rushing adrenaline. From a young age we are taught to 'play every ball on its merits' and that premeditation is not a foundation stone upon which successful batting is built. But as you grow and learn about the game, you acquire the skill of intuiting where the bowler is likely to bowl and planning your retaliation accordingly.

I had planned to give myself a chance by getting in, knowing I would score more freely and catch up on lost balls once settled. At 1–90, we were in an excellent position to launch. But throughout our first fielding effort, I brooded on my undefeated 23 off 37. I would need to accelerate as soon as possible. Taking guard again, I did not leave the dark thick scratch that it had in the morning. With the moisture out of the wicket, trying to etch into the concrete clay with my front spike was a futile act. It was now a typical Adelaide Oval batsman's paradise, with consistent bounce and pace:

one of life's little pleasures as a batsman.

Despite the improved conditions, Cossie and I struggled to make an impact in the five-over power play. I wanted to be playing good cricket shots rather than heaves, and struck a crisp straight drive for four, but then struggled to hit their well executed change-ups, attempting to swing too hard or with too much movement around the crease. I did manage to crunch a low, flat-batted slog, but only as far as my partner's belly.

We went from rotating to dawdling in a matter of balls when Cossie was bowled for a well-made 61. As Bails was making the long walk out from the makeshift change rooms in the Bradman Stand, my thoughts became clouded. Do I try to tee-up while he settles, or do I keep scratching around with only 17 overs to play? I had battled away all day with glimpses of fluency but little rhythm. I asked Bails. 'Just keep rotating', he said. 'You are playing well.' A polite fib, I thought. I was succumbing to what cricketers call 'change room pressure' – the type you feel emanating from your teammates that is actually all in your own head. I was lucky. Bails struck 51 sweet runs from 31 balls, making a fool of me in the process, as I added just 10 runs. He did, however, sweep away my fear and insecurity. By the time he was out, I felt like I'd been sprinkled with magic batting dust. My last 25 came off ten balls, whereupon I was run out by a direct hit with just five overs to play. My 75 off 91 – it had felt like I had consumed almost double that – turned out to be the game's highest score. I had now made three half centuries in my last four one-day innings. Little stats like that can lift you, especially if, like me, you've always been typed as a dour accumulator.

More important than any personal battle with the bat was the result of the game, which today was heavily in our favour. All the bowlers built pressure after a brilliant start by Luke Butterworth, who knocked over their top order with some excellent 'hit the seam' bowling. By the time we had taken three wickets in their second power play the game was done and dusted. The Tigers are on track.

Tuesday, 19 October

A rare chance to be normal and spend some time with my ever-understanding wife. Would I be so compassionate were she away for weeks at a time following her dream? I would like to think so, but somewhere deep down my instinct suggests she is a better person than I am. We're off tomorrow for another nine days ...

At least I can console my perennially suffering 'cricket widow' with the knowledge I am doing this for a living. Yes, it is my passion, but luckily it is also currently paying our bills (not though that it ever feels like a job). More so, I feel heavily for her female comrades, who see their beloveds trudge off for a weekend's club cricket, smiling ear to ear, having worked a full week. The wives and girlfriends of these lovers of the game have had one eye on the forecast all week – their fingers crossed for rain – hoping and praying a sudden deluge will destroy all hopes of a game and grant them some much-needed family time.

Wednesday, 20 October

Groundhog Day? Another lugging of bags around airports, on and off coaches, waiting to check in, sitting on planes, reading the newspapers or what ever else can entertain the mind for more than 20 min. Another inedible plane meal – I might start packing my own. Although it is only one flight when travelling to Sydney (our one-day game is on Friday night), it is still a five-hour ordeal door to door and the day has slipped by. I do feel for many of the poor souls who have to travel on our planes in and out of Hobart. More often than not, our large weight of team baggage means that their luggage is bumped onto the next plane out of town and they are left without a change of clothes for a few hours at their new destination.

I do enjoy the normalness of playing in Sydney. I go home to have a cup of tea and a cuddle with my mum, can grab Dad's car or have dinner with old friends who don't care how many runs I've scored lately. It is still a new experience for me travelling as a tourist to a city that I know so well. Playing against my old teammates certainly 'weirded me out' a little last season. Do I regret not moving sooner? Part of me says yes, but I do think I am glad I moved when I felt I had exhausted all possible options and energies trying to play well for NSW. It allowed me to leave with no regrets – no 'what ifs'. Had I stayed, I suspect I would still be a fringe player – it's by no means certain I would even have a contract. So fond as I am of my old home town, I can also argue that leaving it was among my best decisions.

Thursday, 21 October

A breakfast reunion started my day; a date with two men who have shaped my career more than they would know. Both Patrick Farhart, 'The Godfather' of modern cricket physiotherapy, and Andrew May, perhaps the first in the current generation of strength and conditioning coaches, were both working for New South Wales cricket when I first entered the realms of professional cricket.

At the time, attempting to juggle my last year of undergraduate university and a job in an investment bank with full-time cricket commitments, it is fair to say I was a little naive as to what professional sport involved, both physically and mentally. In such a settled squad with so many senior players – Brad Haddin, Stu Clark, Stuart MacGill, Nathan Bracken and Simon Katich – the cocky 22-year-old got the shit kicked out of him. Looking back, he probably deserved it. Pat and Andrew, although tough on me, took me under their wing. Very quickly I learned the value of punctuality, honesty, and how to grow a thick skin in a pretty masculine micro community. Male sports teams are an unusual, unleavened environment. There is little or no female influence to balance out the testosterone, competitiveness and constant search for alpha male dominance. It can be a tough existence for non-conformists. Sometimes, depending on the culture, individuality is seen as an undesirable trait. There is little slack between being yourself and being viewed as a non team player.

In hindsight, NSW weren't as good as they should have been in match-day preparation. One of the reasons

Tasmania have enjoyed so much success in one-day cricket is that our planning is second to none. We have, through meticulous research, discovered and discussed our preconditions to success. NSW held team meetings, but they were often dominated by the coach and the captain, and lacking in detail. It's a point of pride with the Tigers that we are constantly finding room for improvement. Although we are two from two, today's discussion was democratic and trenchant. We have taken 20 wickets including three direct-hit run-outs – which we know are crucial indicators – but have yet to have someone score over 80, or develop a match-winning partnership. Travis Birt, a hard hitter on and off the field, today quite rightly talked of our poor second power play against SA. It was directed at me, and he was right: I pointed out in response only that we did not lose a wicket, allowing us to back end our innings. The important thing was the spirit of the criticism. It was not about putting me down but the team improving. It showed our strength as a group.

Again I had a poor net session. I have always prided myself on how I train, but somehow it is becoming less of an indicator of how I am travelling. My movements were sluggish and length decisions poor. I consoled myself with the thought of last week, when I was reminded again that training is not the contest – it's interesting how you can redirect negative sensations with positive thoughts when you're in the right frame of mind.

Friday, 22 October

Tasmania 7–286 (Cowan 131, Birt 87) defeated NSW 214 (Doherty 3–35, Krejza 3–55)

The SCG for many years was my second home. Playing out of the visitors change rooms is still very foreign. There is no better place to appreciate this great cricketing venue than from the middle, looking back at the members' grandstand, the city skyline visible from behind the majestic clock.

Despite the familiarity of surroundings and opposition, I was rattled for the entire warm-up – nerves I assumed, but ones that had me on edge. The type that make you deeply introspective, not the butterflies in the stomach that make you talk really quickly. In hindsight I think they were caused by a combination of wanting to do well against my old team, but also from wanting to perform in front of my family and close friends that had come out to watch – as though success today would give justification for putting selfish ambition above their love and friendship. Sometimes the silliest of suggestions are the best. It turns out Bailey and Birt were also suffering from bouts of anxiousness. One of them suggested the medicinal properties of dance. And so, three fully dressed and padded-up cricketers, locked themselves in the back room, the telecast on a small TV and the stereo blaring, jiving and bopping as though they were teenage girls at a sleepover – an odd sight indeed for any fly on the wall. The nerves had been turned into laughter and the freedom of limbs.

Cossie skied one in the eighth over, but we had made a solid start. I misread the length of my first delivery, played back, and left a ball that skimmed past the top of the off bail. Indeed a game of inches. How different my day would have been if the ball had bounced a centimetre less. 'Get forward, make them push you back' was my mid-over self talk.

The question I'm most often asked as an opening batsman is: 'What is it like facing Brett Lee?' The answer is that it's exhilarating. Having seen the rhythmical beast so many times on television as a teenager, to do it live feels strangely like you have done it before, many, many times over. Yes, he is quick, but Brett gives you a great look at the ball in his action. It is important to just let go and trust you will react to the ball coming down at you, calling on your innate survival instinct to protect you from harm. You also feel as though you have nothing to lose. If he sneaks a searing yorker under your bat before you jam it down, you would not be the first; if he bounces you out, he has done it to better.

We were 3–76 at our break, having lost George to the penultimate ball of the session. I was 24 off 40 balls – I had been full of intent, but with an outfield slowed by sand and a clever field placing of a deepish fourth slip, I had been deprived of my reliable glide to third man. With five overs to play their first innings, they passed our score one down, with Brad Haddin in destructive form. Our spinners, as they do so often, wrestled the momentum back and they finished just 16 runs ahead. The game could have been blown apart, but we held our nerve, sensing a turning point.

Following the previous day's talk, I was determined to be more aggressive in the power play – I had to be if we were a chance of winning the game. Despite losing a wicket third ball, I took it upon myself to take a few calculated risks; ones I don't think the opposition were expecting. Growing up playing on a slow Sydney Uni wicket, I had learnt to clear my front leg and slog over midwicket with regularity. For some time though I had lost this shot – tonight, it all came flooding back. Five times in the next five overs I used the depth of my crease to hoick yorkers to the boundary. Travis and I put on 100 in 15 overs – running well, picking gaps and exploiting only four men in the deep. I hit a physical wall in the 80s such was our volume of running on the beachy outfield, but once past 100 found a second wind and accelerated nicely. Our end total of 286 meant we had scored 210 in the second 25 overs. Travis had blazed 87 off 60, and I finished with 131 not out, culminating in a ridiculous reverse lap off the back of the bat to a Brett Lee reverse swinging yorker. Having manipulated his length and field throughout the over, and knowing he had exhausted his other options for a dot ball, I predicted the delivery correctly and was so confident I could execute something I don't even practise.

Bails hit the stumps to run out Haddin, and very quickly the run rate required rocketed to 9 an over for the last 15. Xavier then trapped Phil Jaques LBW for 96, and the spinners reeked havoc with the incoming batsmen, at one stage taking 4–1.

Such a sweet victory, considering how far behind we were at halfway. Seldom have I heard the team song sung with such gusto. We have now won nine of our last 11 one-day games. We stayed as a group of seven or eight back at the hotel, feeding off each other's excitement, watching an old movie re-run, gulping a few frosties, joking and bantering in self-indulgent tones. We are a close team becoming closer. Moments like these make the game's tribulations worth enduring. To experience the full cycle of the day, from sickening nerves right through to the sense of great accomplishment ... the chance of that is what gets me out of bed each morning. Today has been one of the sweetest days in my career from both a team and personal perspective. I am wise enough now, too, to know that a levelling moment is never too far away, but for that knowledge not to spoil the enjoyment of the occasion.

Sunday, 24 October

Still pleasantly weary in the mind, but with a body screaming for attention after a big innings, fielding in the sand, and a short flight, the last 24 hours has involved a huge recovery focus. We play a Sheffield Shield game against Victoria tomorrow at the MCG. They have been the benchmark of domestic four-day cricket for some time. I have never scored big runs at the G. It can be a tough wicket. Early it can be moist and seamy; when dry, it is slow, low-bouncing and hard to score on – one the Victorians know how to exploit. In my career, I've never even experienced a draw here, let alone taken away any points from a fixture.

Monday, 25 October
Tasmania 9–315 vs Victoria

It has been an even first day. Mark Cosgrove blazed a superb 157, while no one else managed 50. We had two 100-run partnerships but neither really took the game away from the opposition.

Cossie, in his debut first-class innings for his adopted home, was nothing short of sublime. When playing against him over the years, we always thought we were a chance to play on his patience. Today, he left the ball with acute judgment. We also used to target his ribs, thinking he was a little susceptible to the shorter, aggressive stuff that tests your character and willingness to fight. The Victorian attack, at full throttle for the entire day, tried this (among other things) for little reward. It was proof Cossie has come a long way and has matured significantly as a player – comfortable in his own skin to do what comes naturally. It seems that a ready-made Test player has dropped into our laps. It was one of the great first-class innings I have seen. Our team has a totally different complexion with his presence.

It could have been a lot worse. We were 3–24, on a wicket providing some assistance. Alex Doolan and Travis also played with great skill. Damien Wright, a wily competitor, swung the ball prodigiously, and had great support from Darren Pattinson, a late bloomer, who was coming off 8–34 at the WACA, and Peter Siddle, pushing again for Australian Test selection. The letdown was that our great fightback ended in a whimper, with the loss of 5–42 either side of the new ball, a bad habit we have slipped into in recent games.

I managed 6, clipping a ball that got a little stuck in the wicket to forward square leg. I was hungry and in the moment – some days are simply not meant to be, and all you can do to console yourself is eat copious amounts of food and attempt the crossword. Any further analysis and I feel I will jeopardise my current mojo.

Tuesday, 26 October

Tasmania 326 vs Victoria 8–261 (Butterworth 4–36)

Very rarely are the Victorians put under pressure when they play in Melbourne. The wicket, an experiment by the groundsman in an attempt to revive the Test playing surface from its current feather-bed status, has so far been a ripper, producing pace, seam and today some big gripping turners sent down by Xavier.

After an inauspicious start by the quickies, our left-arm spinner claimed both openers at bat pad. On the day of his long-overdue ODI call-up, he bowled virtually unchanged from one end throughout the middle and final sessions, controlling the pace of the game and shutting down the scoring. Shane Warne always talked about either bowling defensively with attacking fields or alternatively bowling attacking lines with defensive fields. It was the latter approach that worked for us today – in the vital 40–60 over period, which is usually when runs start to leak and momentum shifts, we slowed them to a walk. The highlight of Doey's five wickets was a ball that drifted onto middle and leg and hit the top of Andrew McDonald's off stump. We continue to win the big moments – none bigger than Bails hitting the stumps (again!) to run out David Hussey. The day twisted and turned with a late-order rally, but we certainly have our noses in front. The Vics know how to bury opponents if given the chance. Such is their efficiency, you can wonder after the game where it was lost and not be able to come up with an answer. They have not lost here for three years; we have not won here for 13. That might just be about to change.

Wednesday, 27 October

Tasmania 326 and 9–226 (Birt 68) vs Victoria 276

The game is set up to have a cracking conclusion – there is no better spectacle in cricket than the last-hour finish after days of toil and sustained effort. We are currently 270 or so ahead on a wicket that is still offering assistance for the new ball as well as taking turn. If we can take a couple of early wickets and put their stroke-making middle order under some pressure, we will be in with a great chance of a historic win. Conversely, if we have a bad hour or session, the game may slip from our grasp.

Our 50-run lead offered us the chance to bury the Vics, but we faltered, reeling at 5–90 shortly after lunch. Peter Siddle, trying to prove his fitness for the first Test, bowled as quick a live spell as I have seen. Hostile, aggressive fast bowling is a joy to watch and even better to face. An adrenaline rush that usually creates pure thoughts and movements – innate instincts come to the fore. A false movement or doubt can result in serious injury – as it did today for young Steve Cazzulino, who, playing his second game, ducked his head on a lifter and took one on the glove that shattered his hand.

Little did he know he was caught in the middle of a rare spell of bowling and first-class cricket is seldom that fearsome. Travis Birt and the lower order held it together nicely until the second new ball, where we lost 3 for 1 to again let them back into the game.

My MCG four-day curse continues: I managed just 12. I deserve a hefty kick up the arse for an overambitious cover drive – with only two days before format changes, it was as though I was still in one-day mode. When I play well in four-day cricket, I build slowly. Today I ran well before I was even preparing to walk, gifting my wicket to the bowler, which I'm simply not a good enough player to do.

I'm not quite a compulsive cover driver in the way that some players become compulsive hookers, but I have a fetish for it. Of the ten shots I best remember from my first-class career, I reckon a solid majority would be drives through the off side; it probably forms a solid majority of my ten most disappointing dismissals too. There is hardly, of course, a more majestic shot in the game; it's the only one where the body is balanced and still at impact, and where your own bat speed and pace on the ball combine most pleasingly. Growing up I tried to mimic the Allan Border flay, sinking then rising with the bounce of the ball. You can manufacture a cover drive – after all, it does not have to be that full to attempt it. But precisely because it is their cover drives that have distinguished many great batsmen, you tend to want to chance it for the wrong reasons – because you want to assert yourself, because you want to feel the surge of control it gives you, because you want to prove that you have what it takes.

As a youngster, I played it well and a lot, because as a left-hander the ball was constantly travelling across me, and I had plentiful opportunities. As the bowlers got faster and the wickets got bouncier, my success rate diminished and eventually I learned its perils in the game's longer forms. In one-day cricket, you have to hit through the ball; more often than not in first-class cricket, the best shot of all is not to offer one. But I can't quite give the cover drive up altogether, because when I'm grooved and in control, there is just no better feeling to be had. What I have to face up to is that, as is meant to be the first step on an addict's reform, I have a problem – a problem I am serious enough as of tonight to confess in print. Part of the reason I started this diary is because I felt it would enhance my accountability to myself. Can't back off now. Luckily my teammates have carried me this game – not contributing in a game hurts all the more if you lose. Oddly, sitting here writing, I pine for a chance to make amends. Where was this desperation when I was batting?

Thursday, 28 October

Tasmania 326 and 234 defeated Victoria 276 and 261 by 23 runs

An incredible game of cricket was played out at the MCG and thankfully it was the Tassie boys who held their nerve to record a monumental win. In a time when T20 cricket seems to hold all the supposed aces – tomorrow, in fact, the CA board are meeting to ratify a new T20 competition – today's Shield game would have been a joy for the purists. As the day unfolded, ebbing and flowing, I always felt we would win. Not to say there were moments that tested this belief. 2–60 at lunch quickly became 4–80. Hussey seemed like the key wicket. He is such a destructive player. In my former life in NSW, he made a habit of fourth-innings hundreds to win games off his own bat. He is the only batsman I ever saw at the SCG make Stuart MacGill look pedestrian. Bailey almost ran him out again, just missing the stumps – 'I hope that does not cost us the game' he muttered. Fortunately, Butterworth took an inside edge and the Vics were at 5–90 odd with two new batsmen at the crease. Sensing the fight had been kicked out of them, we then had a poor hour in the field. Wade and Quiney both gave chances under 10 that were not taken and preceded to get in as the ball got softer. Both streaky at times, they put on 100, and just after tea, Victoria needed 100 runs in 30 overs. I put down a tough chance in the gully – the worst feeling in the game – that would have cracked the game open.

Although on the scoreboard the match was slipping – they needed 60 in 15 overs; we needed five wickets – the feeling on the field was positive. One wicket before the second new ball and I thought we would win. The Vics, too, sensed the big moment – they must have felt runs would come with a lot more ease against the spinner with an old ball and tried to take a few risks. Doherty cleverly left open a huge gap at cover for the left-handed Wade, who drove at a widish half volley and squeezed it to Cosgrove at first slip. Rarely do big partnerships ever finish the game. A wicket in the next over with Wright attempting a huge heave, and all of a sudden the game had turned on its head; 45 runs to win, 12 overs and three wickets required. Another wicket the following over with the second new ball, and in the blink of an eye we had taken 3 for 3. Now the onus was on them and Quiney was last out trying to farm the strike. We had won a thrilling game.

In years gone by, such a monumental win would have prompted wild celebrations and the consumption of copious amounts of booze – initially in the change room and then at any late-night establishment that would have you. Some of my finest cricketing memories involve sitting in the sheds until security, wanting to go home to their families, finally kick you out. On such nights, young players hear war stories of all shapes and ages, with teammates opening up and revealing so much more to each other than they normally would during daylight hours. For better or worse, the game has changed. Needless to say, each and everyone in the room today was filled with contentment and satisfaction of a terrific job well done. As a group, though, we made a commitment: we were playing again in two days' time and needed to control our desire to celebrate wildly. I was one of the last ones home at 10.30 pm with four light beers under my belt – very tame indeed. There will be times to let our hair down, but tonight was just not one of them.

Friday, 29 October

Although at the moment there is quite a high turnover of players from our four-day to one-day team, I do think we sometimes overtrain. We spent three hours at the MCG today, having been there all day, every day for the past week. Having said that, it is completely player driven, so I can't really complain. Even if the session was non-compulsory, I think everyone would turn up and prepare exactly the same way. There seems to be no viable alternative. By the time you've been to the nets, done a recovery session and had a massage, your day off has soon slipped away and you have been reduced to trivial duties like washing your clothes.

Saturday, 30 October

Victoria 2–112 vs Tasmania 1–9 (match abandoned due to rain)

Some kind of meteorological Armageddon had been predicted for today – over 45 mm of rain in five hours. Rain seems the order of the summer so far. We played, albeit briefly, and as though the weatherman's predictions had a history of exactness. Mentally, we were off right from the get-go. I've often thought a lot can be told about a team from how they warm up – like a galloper in the dress ring before a big race, punters swarm to see how their favourite horse looks on the day. Nervous? Flustered? Jerky? Relaxed? Today, it was in our eyes and in our actions that we did not expect to play for very long and were sloppy because of it. Usually precise in our attention to detail, we looked like a herd of lost sheep. Reduced games do occur – we almost cost ourselves a finals place last season by blowing up in a 17-over fixture. Despite the possibility of a similar situation, we again failed to adapt.

The eventual rain – and the 2 points – were a real let-off.

We tend to stick together on the last night of tours – our last chance to be boys before the reality of being husbands and dads kicks in at the airport the next day. Conversation last night quickly turned to T20 cricket and the announcement on late Friday of the new expanded Big Bash to take place next year. We all had had 24 hours to digest it and all kinds of unanswered questions arose over the dinner table. Where will the two new teams be based? Will players be drafted or recruited on free agency? The latter would undoubtedly be a better outcome for players' bank accounts, but would result in more player movement. For me, this is a huge hurdle to the competition's success. Cricket Australia's 'research' has shown the public not caring for traditional state allegiances – I find this hard to swallow. It feels as though they are building a made-for-Indian-television product. Here lies my concern: sports passion and tribalism of support are all built around the sensory experience of actually being present at the game. People have over the years fallen in love with a day at the cricket and the joy it brings. The loud crowd murmur of expectation; the eruption of emotion that can sweep you off your chair and etch itself into your memory when you witness what is collectively recognised as a special moment. The Steve Waugh last ball hundred, Warney's 300th wicket, Bevo's 4 to win – these were all moments that I saw live that helped shape my love of the game.

The competition, it seems, will make money regardless, and in doing so create huge new revenue streams (ironically for non-profit organisations), but profitability should not be the sole judge of success. If I sound a reluctant supporter, I am not. I am a pragmatic traditionalist. It pains me to see players like Keiron Pollard become rock stars of a generation. But I accept that growing the game and making it sustainable for future generations to fall in love with has to be a priority of administrators. I am excited, but I just fear that the romanticism of cricket could well have died in the process.

Monday, 1 November

I think since coming home from Holland a little over two months ago, I've spent seven or eight days in my own bed. Little pleasures such as cooking dinner or reading on your own couch have begun to feel like sinful luxuries. After a gym session and a massage, I adjourned to watch the Second XI at Bellerive – mainly to see how the pitch was playing in its first outing of the year. There is some talk around our group that the wicket is going to be juiced up to give our four fast bowlers the best opportunity of 20 wickets.

We now have a good run of games at home and above all else, it was great to be able to unpack my cricket kit back into my locker at Bellerive. The change room becomes our second home during the season, and to feel settled in there does provide a simple comfort. Because Bellerive seldom hosts a Test, the décor is Tiger-centric; the walls are painted in green, red and yellow stripes and adorned with photos of teams celebrating great wins throughout the ages. Upon walking in, you are greeted with a prominent honour board hosting the inscriptions of Tasmanian records: if one is ever broken, we take great pride in using a yard of physio tape and a permanent marker to ensure they are up to date. My dressing room space, usually a bit of a mess, is in a much sought-after location – near the window and TV, and close enough to the coffee machine that you can smell a freshly brewed cup. Sadly it is too far away from the stereo to really affect the play list, but that is something else I am working on.

Tuesday, 2 November

To prepare for Saturday's one-day game against Queensland, George and I had a light hit together – something we usually both get a lot from. We train well together; we are honest in our assessment of each other and tend to feed off each other's competitiveness in these kinds of sessions. Bails is struggling for runs by his lofty standards – I think the whisper of him being in the mix for higher honours this summer may be weighing him down. But he looks close to cracking his summer open with a big score.

It is odd that we gel so well – usually players of similar styles migrate to each other for throw-down practice. As players, we are stroke-making chalk (George) and blocking cheese (me). George is the most natural of players you are ever likely to see – Australia's answer to AB De Villiers. His best is world class, and in my opinion he is the outstanding one-day player in the land. His worst, however, can be diabolical, coming usually when he overanalyses and stifles his naturalness. I imagine it can be hard for him sometimes – the captain has to be seen so often to be doing the right thing, and particularly at Bellerive where faulty techniques can get exposed, he feels obligated to go searching for answers. In contrast, my best and worst are not that far apart – it is just that my best is not seen often enough. If things are not working for me technically, I tend to know what is wrong without too much thought. I could do with some of his ease, and he could do with some of my ability to dissect my own game.

The selection of the Australian A team next week is distracting us both a little; perhaps, if I'm honest, it has been on my mind for a few weeks. It can be hard to differentiate between wanting something so much that it clouds your thoughts, and harnessing that same desire to drive you to get the most out of yourself. Not a day goes by that I don't daydream of playing Test cricket. Fortunately, perhaps, because I'm down the pecking order, it's an inspiration rather than a distraction. The A team is different. Having played a part in the A series in the winter and tasted some success, I can feel its closeness.

It is most likely between Shaun Marsh and myself to partner Phil Hughes at the top of the order. I'm almost glad in a sense that there is not another Shield game before selection. My cards have been played – sadly more so in one-day cricket this season – and I can only pray that I have a few credits in the bank. To play against the Poms one game before the first Test would not only be an incredible challenge; to succeed would undoubtedly fast-track international ambitions. In the meantime, though, I must only play one ball at a time.

Thursday, 4 November

I had an invigorating one-on-one session today on the outdoor turf wickets with Diva. He has brought a 'side-arm winder' back from the UK – a type of ball-flicker that would look more at home with your dog on the beach but that generates great pace and bounce, in addition to saving his shoulder from wear and tear (a common coach's curse). I was sharp, physically and mentally; clear headed, reacting with purpose to the ball coming down, and playing with conviction off both feet. I don't think I could've played any better – great weight through the ball, playing it late and straight. A big score is around the corner if I can recreate this same intensity in the middle. After all the one-day cricket practice, it was great to get back to a red ball focus, leaving well, and getting my head around constructing a big innings.

We also had an excellent full squad review for an hour or so – the first time all 20 or so squad members have been in the same room since the start of the season. I think squad morale can always be judged by how loved the peripheral members feel. The coaching staff and leadership group have done an excellent job in making our recent success about the whole squad and not just the 11 on the field. Interestingly, ladders of all six teams based on our winning performance targets were presented to us. No surprise that we lead the competition in boundary percentage of runs and percentage of scoring shots, while we also ranked high in our bowling economy and fielding effectiveness. We ate dinner together in the players' dining room and then had a 90-minute fielding session under lights. Despite the cold (about 9 degrees when the sun goes down), we trained with purpose and precision.

Xavier Doherty made his one-day international debut today in Melbourne and made a little bit of a mockery of his previous lack of selection, taking four wickets against Sri Lanka, who staged a magnificent comeback win against a fragile Australian team. When I started playing for NSW, such was the monotony of players going off to play for Australia, it was referred to simply as them 'being away for the week'. It's a much bigger deal here – and X is one of the good guys.

Friday, 5 November

We had a light top-up team session before tomorrow's one-day game and again I felt technically at the top of my game – back to punching my drives with control and balance. I need to make sure that I take nothing for granted and don't just assume it's going to happen for me tomorrow. Perhaps my only concern at the moment is my body, which has been playing a few tricks on me lately – I must be getting old.

I do think that successful and thoughtful athletes are part performance psychologist, part physiologist. They understand their bodies, their limits, their susceptibilities, their needs. At 28, I'm no longer bulletproof. I'll need to listen to my body more if I'm to make the most of what cricket I have left in me.

Saturday, 6 November
Tasmania 5–168 defeated Queensland 9–167

Sunday, 7 November

Tasmania cruised to our tenth victory in our last 12 one-dayers tonight without really needing to get out of second gear. Our new ball bowlers swung the ball prodigiously, and Queensland eked out just 5 runs in the first six overs. I doubt we will put in a better bowling performance. Our quicks – Denton, Hilfenhaus and Drew – were all sublime. In the field we hit the stumps six times and inflicted 30 overs of dot balls on our opponents, which in turn caused hurried and panicky shots in the middle order. At one stage it looked as though there would be no need to turn on Bellerive's lights, but they finally gave us a target, which we knocked off with 15 overs to spare. Tim Paine, having just returned from the Test tour of India, scorched 70 off as a many balls, while George, despite being hopelessly nervous while waiting to bat, an aggressive 50. There is a special feeling of togetherness among the group – the celebrations were warm and relaxed.

I was fucking hopeless with the bat, managing 1 before nicking a back-foot push – an absolute waste of time and effort for everyone involved in helping me prepare for the game, leaving me with that empty feeling of regret and nothingness. Was I watching the ball? Was I too relaxed? Did I not prepare well enough mentally? I was flabbergasted at my own ineptness and inability to compete. It is about time I started batting in the middle like my career depended on it. If I want to be the player I think I can be, it is time to stop treading water and start getting out there and doing it. Perhaps this diary is indeed an incubus – less than two weeks ago I was on top of the world. Fewer words, more actions please Ed, it is time to lift. This coming week, including the first of three Shield games without a break, must be a fresh start.

Monday, 8 November

A new day has produced a clear head – partly from writing last night and partly from just letting go of the disappointment I felt. Intensity at training was lifted significantly purely though the presence of Ricky Ponting, who will be playing the next two Sheffield Shield games with us. It can be an awkward introduction when one of the big boys enters the change room. You throw out a hand and say hi, but how do you respond to 'Hi, I am Ricky'? You know full well who it is, you are a little excited by the whole moment, and you don't know how much you should draw out the conversation. 'Is that with a "y" or "ie"?'

Not that I was expecting him to go through the motions, but I was blown away by the intent with which he trained. From warm-up throws right through to his batting rituals, the man did absolutely everything with a purpose. It was a valuable lesson for anyone who witnessed it. He grabbed me to warm up his shoulder – a basic 'play catch' scenario, where you both throw to each other's baseball mitts from about 20 metres. Humorously, I had been struggling with the momentary yips when throwing to a glove for a week or so, pelting balls over the head and wide of who ever the poor sod was who had to play with me, forcing them often to turn and chase. Ricky's first throw thundered into my glove with pinpoint accuracy. Like a golfer standing over a 2-foot putt, I took a deep breath and, inspired by the Australian captain waiting for the return offering, threw the ball back as hard as I could. Thanks be to the god of cricket, it rocketed into his glove.

I had heard stories of how giving of himself Ponting is, but he threw balls at Bails for hours, coached and offered advice, and was generally available and involved. It was uplifting.

I had an excellent training day, not taking my pads off for hours. Initially batting against the bowlers each with a new ball in their hand and then again with Diva at the end. I was focusing on my routines more than anything – taking my time between each ball, replicating the timing of a match and getting in the headspace of batting long periods with the discipline I will need on Wednesday.

The wicket in the middle has 10 centimetres of fresh, live grass on it, but is as hard as a rock underneath. When Tasmania won the Shield four seasons ago, the wickets looked a lot like this one – a good sign for a result in the game but not a great sign for an opening batsman hungry for runs. Moments like these raise the question of the recurring tension between personal ambition and team achievement. To overcome the urge of selfish desire, you need to remind yourself that you play a team game and you play to win. I would be happy if the wicket was like this all year as it means we will be a chance to win the Shield, even if it might cost me some runs. Runs without team success has always seemed to me the most sterile of achievements – if I'm good enough, it shouldn't matter what surface I play on.

Tuesday, 9 November

If you ever see the Chairman of Selectors' number come up on your phone, in my experience it's best not to answer. Very rarely is it good news. There is the odd occasion that you are willing and praying for that phone call, and the sense of vindication has you yelling, screaming or dancing around your kitchen. Last night, however, there was no such luxury. I was stuck in a communication black hole, having had my phone stolen at the local shopping centre. On any normal day, this would have been an annoyance, but last night it caused huge anxiety. The Australian A team was being selected. I had no way to find out if I was in or if I was out; selection limbo hell.

Honest cricketers usually have a sixth sense for these kinds of issues. I knew deep down that if I was selected, I would be good enough not to just be a passenger but dominate a day's play if things went my way. I also knew from experience that selectors don't always hold the same view as the individual in question. It turned out my gut feel was correct. When finally I learned the team, Shaun Marsh had gotten the nod.

Out of professional pride, I feel as though I would have done a better job than Marsh, a very good player not at the top of the order in four-day cricket. He's scored two first-class hundreds in the last three years (and three in the last six seasons); I've made four in my last 12 games. Perception is often reality when it comes to selection. Throughout my career, even as a junior, I have battled against a perception that a kid who went to a good school and had a degree must be as soft as butter. The irony is that I haven't had advantages. I bumped into David Boon, a national selector among other things, before training at Bellerive, and quizzed him about the selection – I am at an age that I am not going to die wondering by just going with the flow. He told me I was in the thoughts of the selectors and that weight of runs was a powerful currency, but the other two (Marsh and Phil Hughes) were 'in the system' – meaning centrally contracted to Cricket Australia – and that this was a driving force of selection. My upbringing and education in any other walk of life would make me an insider. In Australian cricket, it leaves me an outsider. And so be it. I am happy to look after my own game and make my own way. Learning of my non-selection left me feeling strangely happy and resolved and I trained with deep intent, batting with authority and purpose. I feel prepared, a little anxious and more than ready for the challenges of tomorrow.

Wednesday, 10 November

Tasmania 4–120 vs Queensland – rain delay (Cowan 30)
In thick overhead conditions of grey rain clouds and mountain mist, and a pitch that had a thick layer of live, furry grass, whoever won the toss was destined to bowl: at 10.15 I was strapping the pads on. When the third ball from Ryan Harris nipped back 30 centimetres and cannoned into Jon

Wells' front pad, the suggestion of it being a tricky day's batting seemed somewhat of an understatement.

Then – the big moment. As a teenager, I had a poster of RT Ponting above my bed (only for it to be replaced with Joey from *Dawson's Creek* in later years). Now here we were batting together. Looking down the wicket was almost like watching television, so familiar was I with the technique and mannerisms of my esteemed partner. It was remarkably comfortable. I did catch myself a few times hamming it up as though we'd been lifelong teammates – 'Great shot Punter, keep going mate, next ball now' – but such was his inviting aura, I felt I had been.

Looking down at a wicket resembling an unshorn sheep, hearing the murmurs of the five or six fielders behind the wickets and facing a bowler in Harris proving his fitness for Test selection was otherwise a daunting prospect. Several balls kicked and thundered into my ribs, knocking the wind out of me. Rarely is opening the batting easy per se, but also is it rarely this full-on. It was all about surviving the Harris onslaught, the pace, the movement, the aggression. I stayed positive, observing the old adage, 'Never look back once the ball passes you at the crease'. I had no interest in seeing a keeper 25 metres back having to dive in every direction to stop the ball rocketing to the fence.

I also wanted the contest and had a steely resolve to win it. Before the game I had made a promise with myself to be absolutely meticulous with my routine; a tap, two deep breaths, and then two more taps before the ball was released. In times of pressure, falling back onto something as familiar as this provides the mind and body with assurance. You have done it before and you get can through it. After a while I felt in a state almost trance-like, not thinking about my hands or feet – just the ball. It was nice to have the time to get there, which one-day cricket does not offer.

Having batted for nearly 120 balls, I fell trying to defend a ball that nipped across me prodigiously. It felt like I had done virtually nothing wrong – I could have left it on length but certainly not line. It had been an innings of satisfying resolve in trying conditions. It may sound a little strange that I was satisfied considering the nothingness of my score – the game can sometimes transcend the scorecard and I certainly felt I could not have played any better. A start like this would normally infuriate me – there is little reason to get out in the 30s barring a lack of self-discipline and hunger. But today I was prepared to accept the rub of the green – there being a lot of green to get the rub off. When rain stopped play after 50 overs, it felt like a 50–50 game: 250 would be an excellent first innings score.

Thursday, 11 November – Remembrance Day

Tasmania 196 vs Queensland 9–254 (Maher 3–53)

The wicket settled down after lunch today, by which time unfortunately we were all out. The new ball worked for us – Queensland were 5–80 at one stage, with the good guys making the entire running. But Travis dropped James Hopes at second slip and the game slipped away. Travis has superb hands but is going through one of those phases where nothing sticks. There is certainly nowhere to hide in the cordon and the ball always seems to come when your confidence is down and you least want it to – although the consolation is that confidence is seldom more than one catch away.

When defending a low total like we were, you need a few things to go your way. Two umpiring decisions at important times went against us and they ended up 50 ahead when it could easily have been 50 behind, which on these kinds of wickets is often the difference between winning and losing.

We bowled well in patches, and okay in others, sometimes too wide and generally without luck. Perhaps we are a bowler short, but the three quicks and a spinner served us well in Melbourne. The only difference being here that this wicket is not turning, only allowing Xavier to merely hold up an end, which it must be said he is doing with great aplomb.

Friday, 12 November

Tasmania 196 and 271 vs Queensland 254 and 0–2 (Cowan 65)

Within the space of two balls and ten minutes, Queensland were all out and we were 1–0. Poor old Wellsy did not even get a sighter from Ryan Harris; a pair in his comeback game. I felt for him. We all did. He had fought so very hard to get back into the side after a horrid run of outs last season, plundering anyone brought before him in the second XI and grade cricket, only to be disposed of in the time it takes to boil a kettle. He seems to be in decent form – a pair is no indication otherwise (sounds silly but it is hard to judge form when you don't get a solitary run). His technical flaws of last year seemed to be ironed out and if he starts believing he is good enough, there is no doubt he will prove it in the coming weeks. Ponting also came and went quickly, although again I cherished my one-on-one time with the Test captain – time that was intimate and no one can ever take away from me.

Bails and I scratched initially but then flew through to the over prior to lunch, when George, whose feet had just started to obey his head, nicked an innocuous delivery. We were only 40 ahead and again had handed back the initiative to the visitors. The wicket had flattened considerably, particularly against the older ball. I got in again after lunch and brought up a well-crafted 50. It felt like I was going to bat until the sun went down, such was the headspace I again found myself in. I then pulled a long hop off the leggie straight to the man on short square, there to save the single, almost disbelieving of the offering. Out for 65. It felt like it was going to take something out of the ordinary to dislodge me. It certainly was that, just that it was on the hopeless side of ordinary. I could have hit it anywhere but chose to keep it down, attempting not to be greedy and to do the right thing. Poor option. Luck often favours the brave. One metre up, left or right or down on a field with the vastness of an empty paddock, and it would have been 4. We play a cruel game. It felt far worse than in the first innings.

Looking back on the day's play, it was a turning point. So to were two poor LBW decisions and Tim Paine's decision to try and slog-sweep the spinner the last over before the new ball; out for 70 of the most fluid and graceful runs you are likely to see, but it was a poor shot from an experienced player. The tail crumbled to the new ball and we found ourselves with a lead of 208. Under lights, after a lengthened day, we had the chance to make early inroads with 18 overs still to be bowled in friendly conditions; but the rain came, having threatened to all day. We are going to need early new ball wickets, as otherwise we won't be able to build any scoreboard pressure. I feel we are still a huge chance of victory, but we will need some of the luck that has deserted us so far this game.

Saturday, 13 November

Tasmania 196 and 271 lost to Queensland 254 and 2–214 by 8 wickets

Some days the stars just don't align – catches fall agonisingly short, the batters play and miss, and decisions that could change the game go against you. We had one of those days. Not through lack of trying; it just didn't happen for us. On a now placid wicket, we could not build any prolonged scoreboard pressure. The result suggests Queensland flogged us, but over the four days we lost a few big moments that cost us dearly. One of the beautiful and least understood concepts of our great game is that 'butterfly and hurricane effect' – a dropped catch on day two can affect the outcome late on day four – an effect only ever perceptible in hindsight. This was our first loss of the year. Losing always hurts, but we all agreed we were not that far off the running of the game.

We'll move on, and have to quickly, taking on NSW on Wednesday at the SCG, who are fielding a team stacked with members of the current Test team.

On my way home, I thought about my oldest childhood friend Joey, who I went all the way through school and university with – it was his wedding day – another significant summer event that I have not been able to attend due to my selfish pursuit of a dream. When this career is all over, I will owe a lot of love, understanding, compassion and support to many friends and family member who have been so forgiving of such.

Sunday, 14 November

I woke this morning to a series of missed calls, all from unrecognisable numbers – one of those annoying inconveniences of using a fill-in phone. A sleepy call back quickly turned to alertness when CA selector Greg Chappell answered the phone. Shaun Marsh had hurt his back and I was to replace him in this week's Australia A game in Hobart.

I was excited but also subdued. How your destiny can change in a manner of minutes! I'm now faced with the single greatest opportunity of my career. My situation is a blessed one, I think. The pressure will be on Usman Khawaja and Callum Ferguson to score runs and mount a case for the first Test (particularly the way Mike Hussey has been travelling and the mounting media crusade against him). I am not 'in the system' – so I feel there is no public expectation and thus be playing with nothing to lose.

Monday, 15 November

Preparing for the biggest individual game of my life, I woke up in my own bed and trained at Bellerive like any other game of cricket in Hobart. The familiarity undoubtedly helped me to relax into a new group of teammates – although only so far. At the end of the week my teammates will go back to being rivals. Such one-off games are like that – superficially you play as a team, but little hinges on the overall result.

Talent-wise, there is no doubt we will match it with the Poms, even if they don't rest their front-line bowlers as they have advertised; but they will be a hardened team unit, and the majority of our team will be playing for themselves.

Motivation in sport is a mysterious thing. Some love the contest, some love the money, some are driven by trying to prove people wrong. My greatest single motivation is trying to win for the teammates I care about; to not let them down. I'll have to dig deeper this week because it seems this particular match is all about the individual – maybe the sooner I grasp that reality, the better.

Tuesday, 16 November

I am by no means obsessive-compulsive – or so I think – but at an early age I learned the benefits of routine – blocking out the negativity as familiarity engulfs you and your body relaxes. Batting routines help you out in the middle – the taps, the breaths, the self-talk and ritualistic fidgeting. Today had a macro-routine feel to it. Despite his not being part of the Australian A coaching staff, I had a hit with Diva, ate dinner at one of our usual haunts, wrote notes about opposition bowlers while lying on the couch and generally prepared like it was just another game at Bellerive.

I've caught myself daydreaming a few times, of hundreds and Test matches, but snapped out of it with a realisation that in order to succeed this week, I have to stay in the moment. I am ready, not at all anxious, just a little keyed up, as though I'd like to go to bed now, at 4 pm, so tomorrow would come around just that little quicker.

Wednesday, 17 November

Australia A vs English XI

We lost the toss and the visiting English XI had no hesitation in bowling. The wicket looked like it was going to be tricky for a day, but by no means a minefield. It seems the groundsman did not have the bottle to leave too much in it – groundsmen tend to be fearful of producing 'juicy' wickets in big games for fear of reprisal – and that gave the toss added importance.

I woke up feeling heavy – nerves perhaps – and the normality of the last couple of days soon meant very little. My first 15 balls were the worst I can remember in years. It felt like I had completely forgotten how to hold a bat – not a good time for this to happen. My feet were talking French, my hands Spanish, and my mind was at war with itself. 'This cannot be happening', I thought to myself.

I prodded without conviction at a ball I should have left and nicked it. I turned around quickly enough to see it fly just wide of Paul Collingwood at slip. It shocked and also heartened me, in that way a slice of good fortune can. This was my day – a day a lot of people would be seeing me bat, on television, for the first time. I did not want to embarrass myself. Perception in cricket so easily becomes reality. If I failed now, I would be associated in many viewers' minds with failure: did I want this? When my batting came back to me, it came quickly. Quick enough for me to start soaking up the experience – my own little Test match – sharing jokes with myself and generally relaxing into the day's play.

Wickets tumbled around me and before I blinked I was 28 and we were 3–50. I started thinking that with my start and everyone else faltering, it was my chance for something special – a career-defining innings perhaps. Then, as it so often happens when you think too far ahead, I made half a mistake and was on my way back to the sheds. I pulled a ball strongly but sadly at a catching height, to see, in slow motion from my vantage point, Monty Panesar sticking out a right-hand full of fingers and lunging at the ball like a dog on the beach. It stuck. A catch I doubt even he could fathom. His teammates erupted, partly with laughter. As I was walking off, Channel 9 had obviously shown a replay, and the only thing to catch my attention were the physios and fitness staff rushing out the door of the visitors' change rooms hollering with shock and congratulations.

I had acquitted myself well in tricky conditions when others had faltered a little around me. Around the team, though, I felt little vibe, and my thoughts turned to the Tasmanian game in Sydney. NSW had been bowled out for 93 – incredible. Yet for parts of the afternoon, their first innings total looked insurmountable as we slumped and clawed and then slumped again. At the moment the Tassie team are my family and part of me desperately wanted to be there. Eventually they were dismissed for 120, with late cameos from new Test squad member Doherty, and Luke Butterworth, who is playing with every inch of his laconic talent at present.

Aussie A managed 230 and England lost Andrew Strauss late to be 1–20. The English captain played a lazy drive that flew to gully. It seems I am not the only one with the affliction of not being able to resist temptation! Up close, you realise the big Test players are not as infallible as you imagine. You hear their deep breaths, their moments of insecurities and self-talk. They are mere mortals, like you, and it was reassuring to see at such close proximity. It gave me hope and knowledge that I'm not that far off the running.

Thursday, 18 November

In years gone by, a televised fielding day would have petrified me as I fumbled, fell and tripped my way to embarrassment with hands that invariably felt like bricks, and a throwing arm your sister would not be proud of. Thankfully you are allowed to improve if you so desire and my fielding is no longer such a source of great comedy.

Today belonged to Ian Bell, who played masterfully for a large, unbeaten century. He is obviously a much different player from the last time he was on these shores, and it was clear from the outset that his technique was going to suit the Australian conditions – playing off both feet, making large decisive movements and being ultra positive against spin. Almost humorously, KP was dismissed by a left-arm spinner; undoubtedly his kryptonite. If only the Australians had known this at the Oval in 2005.

The success of our left-arm spinner, Steven O'Keefe, against their middle order may increase the chances of Xavier playing in the first Test, having been a shock inclusion in the squad. This may seem odd for some, but such has been the ineffectiveness of Nathan Hauritz against right-handers, the selectors' hands may be forced. In Sydney, the mighty Tigers need another 90 runs for a remarkable win. I am getting more pleasure watching them from afar than I am from the game I'm meant to be playing.

Friday, 19 November

By the time the English tail had wagged, we found ourselves almost 300 runs adrift and with no hope of winning the game.

I crunched my first ball – a full-blooded cut shot – only to see it stopped by a full-length dive and then the same result occurred an over later when I nailed a pull shot to wide mid-on. Still being on zero after 30 balls is never a nice feeling, but the wicket was good, albeit starting to go a little up and down. Unlike the first innings, my feet were moving and I was batting with conviction. I did not panic, nor feel the inclination to. Thirty balls later I was 30 not out (with four boundaries from pull shots) and it felt like I was truly away.

The pull shot, and more specifically its inclusion in my own game, makes for interesting analysis. For some, the shot is an addiction. Opposing captains can place two in the deep, and they will still go for it. It's an ego shot, for sure – *mano e mano*. I play it. The trouble is I get out to it way too often. At one stage last season, five of seven dismissals came from it, although admittedly I had had a decent run of scores throughout that time. Should I give it up? I can't, really. Opening batsmen who don't play the pull shot rarely make it to the top in my opinion – Test cricket is a back-foot game. What I have to do is play it better and to play it more wisely; to show a willingness to trust my instinct but more importantly to be prepared to grind away without it sometimes. It is certainly a lot easier pulling a tired bowler than a fresh one who is being fuelled by the adrenaline of a new contest.

When Tim Bresnan dug another one in from around the wicket with two back, a square catching mid wicket and a bat pad, I took the shot on, only to drag it on to my off stump. I was livid. Such a wasted opportunity – two starts. In the end, it was the matter of probably an inch. Skill? Luck? Both probably. That's all it takes.

Despite my missed opportunities, I'm sure I will look back on my week with satisfaction some time in the near future. I tried my guts out, although sadly as a batsman we are judged on the result. Why is this sad? I guess it is a reflection of the fact that 'outsiders' have little clue as to the effort that goes into attempting to succeed – the effort of risking failure. That's only natural. I catch myself using the words 'pathetic' when watching sport the whole time, only to remember from my own 'pathetic' moments how hard I have often been trying. It seems bloody hard to earn plaudits in sport, but bloody easy to be labelled no good. Perhaps the biggest insecurity in sport that needs to be overcome is caring about what other people think.

Meanwhile in Sydney, Tasmania recorded a truly remarkable win. A collapse meant the last wicket needed to put on 37 to win the game, which in such a low-scoring affair was virtually impossible. I watched every ball on the live internet streaming during our lunch break, screaming at the computer with support as Adam Maher held up an end while Luke Butterworth attacked. With ten to win, Hauritz dropped a sitter at third slip to help twist an already intriguing plot. Butterworth did not let Maher face another delivery after the last near mishap, swatting 4 then 6 off Doug Bollinger to complete a spectacular win.

By the time I spoke to the guys, they were sprucing themselves up for a BBQ at Punter's house. Jealousy is a curse, I know. There is no reason for him to put on such an event, bar the fact he has clearly loved playing for Tasmania again; there has been no need for him to be as generous and enthusiastic either. We've experienced a measure of the man from what he's done that hasn't been necessary.

Saturday, 20 November

We predictably lost today, but the contagious attitude of individuality meant that no one really minded. My highlight for the day included a lunchtime quip from Kevin Pietersen, who in his high-pitched mixed accent (which could not be less suited to a man of his stature) asked 'What the fuck is this?' as he cast his gaze over the lunch buffet. I mentioned that it was bread and butter pudding and being English he should surely know what that was. 'I am not fucking English Eddie', he joked. 'I am South African, I just work here!' Touché Kevin, touché.

I did manage to have a few quiet beers after the game, and Hobart town being the small port that it is, at the same venue as the opposition. Before too long, members of each team were mingling freely and I was lucky enough to converse with Alastair Cook, who I have now decided is the most unaffected and lovely cricketer I have met throughout my career. Tim Paine, walking past, remarked, 'Don't talk for too long Cookie, he will head fuck you with all his theories'. I was taken aback. Am I the 'theory guy'? Oh dear ...

All in all, it was a week that gave me another insight into the inner workings of the Australian set-up and a few of the cogs that make it go around. But sadly, because it never felt like we were a team, it was a fairly artificial taste. I think a few of the participants were a little upset with how it had all panned out for them. I have never seen Usman so disappointed with himself. Over dinner last night, he confided how disappointed he was that he'd put so much pressure on himself. He has become a master of controlling his emotions, acting with humility and grace regardless of whether he walks off with a duck or a masterful hundred. This rare quality will hold him in great stead for an undoubtedly stellar Test career.

Sunday, 21 November

Tim Paine broke his finger tonight while playing in the gala T20 'All Stars' game in Brisbane. From all reports, he will need a major operation on his right index finger. I am left shaking my head in disbelief that this game still exists on the calendar. It is not the first major injury to emerge from it in recent times. When the concept was first dreamt up by the Australian Cricketers' Association it seemed an ideal way to shake off winter blues and renew public interest in cricket after a long winter hiatus – the Australian team at that time played the best of domestic talent in a game that split the public's allegiances and reminded the big boys that there was a young whippersnapper on their heels, ready and waiting for their job. This year, however, the 'big boys' rested, relegating the game to a glorified net session – at times even that would be giving it an unjustified excitement. Matthew Hayden bowled the last over to ensure a close finish. What a debacle.

I feel for Tim. Having spent the winter in both the Test and one-day teams, this summer was a huge opportunity to continue to press for the top keeping role on a permanent basis. Now, after just two first-class games, he will miss up to two and half months' cricket. From a purely selfish point of view, it is also bad news for the Tigers. I am currently having visions of our coach throwing a tantrum in his living room upon learning the fate of our best player – 'bloody Mickey Mouse game of cricket …'.

Monday, 22 November

The best news to emerge from today is Xavier's inclusion in the Test team – a meteoric rise to say the least. He will be his calm and laid-back self, a major asset for anyone thrust into the limelight as quickly as he has been. There is no doubt he will give his absolute all. The Ashes excitement is building for Thursday. Let's all pray that there is some life in the pitch. My biggest beef with Test cricket, particularly in Australia, has been the lack of assistance for bowlers around the country. The Sydney Test last year, despite the match-fixing cloud it is under, has still been the finest of recent memory.

There will be some criticism of Xavier's selection. His career stats are by no means mind-blowing – in line with my theory (here I go again) that alongside career stats, a 'rolling average' of the last 10 or 15 performances would be useful. Xavier's last ten games (played over two seasons) see him averaging less than 25 with the ball, making him the in-form spin bowler in the country.

In *Moneyball*, Michael Lewis demonstrates that it is the most commonly reported statistics, the ones on which the public and sports writers focus, that are often the ones of least importance. The book was inspired by the success of the Oakland Athletics – a Major League baseball team whose payroll was at times one-fifth that of some of their competitors but who significantly outperformed richer clubs. Their model was based on simple economics – buying assets (players) that had been undervalued by the marketplace. How did they find such value in a market where there is asymmetry of information? They simply came up with a new method of valuation – breaking long-held baseball traditions and, in the process, dismissing the statistics that had been deemed meaningful in valuing players. Their manager Billy Beane worked out that popular stats such as batting average, runs batted in (RBI), fielding errors and stolen bases were largely irrelevant and subjective; lesser-known statistics such as 'on-base percentage' were in fact far better indicators of a player's contribution – more importantly, such qualities that were not valued as highly by the market. He forwent obvious and popular draft picks of the fastest and strongest, for the obscure and obese, based on his own methods of valuation. What emerged was a team of perceived misfits that found ways of winning baseball games.

It has had me thinking that cricket's traditional statistical analysis is in parts archaic and does not give the full picture of one's value to the team. 'How many hundreds does he have?' is an often-heard expression when inquiring about someone's quality. It is relevant, but what you really want to know is what percentage of these were scored in winning matches, how many accounted for over half the team's score in an innings, were they scored overseas and at what stage of a series?

I don't think we as consumers of the game get the information we deserve. Stats don't lie – it is just a question of which stats. You can find confirmation in your belief on any player; it just depends on what your belief is.

To round out my day, I went for a long and therapeutic beach run to keep the body ticking over and my mind fresh – half the battle of getting through a busy year.

Tuesday, 23 November

Another day of non-cricket goodness, although I think I am getting the flu. Not a good time to come down with anything. Rarely do I get through a season without a bout of something. Sometimes I feel as though I should really live in a bubble. I am aching and feverish and don't feel the urge to write.

Wednesday, 24 November

Arrrgghh – sick! I can't even swallow; every effort is like drinking razor blades. I attempted to train but got nowhere and was sent home.

Thursday, 25 November

Day 1 of the Ashes and perhaps the biggest series in my lifetime – I had an excuse to watch every ball from the couch! I am still feeling rubbish. We play tomorrow against South Australia. First-class cricket is hard enough already, let alone without the ability to think straight. It might be good for me to bat without the energy for contemplation.

Friday, 26 November

Tasmania 251 (Doolan 68) vs SA 2–10

We won the toss and batted (a rare event at home) on a Bellerive wicket that looked as though it would be hard work to bat for three or four sessions, but that would turn into a batting paradise later in the game. The decision was perhaps heavily influenced by the saying at Bellerive to 'look up not down' at the toss of the coin – in reference to the fact that overhead conditions play more a part in the decision than the wicket itself. For a change, the sun was out and the day just had that batting feel – it was regarded in the change room as a positive move. We made it otherwise. Wellsy nicked one early and in the process, lifted our season's average opening partnership from under 6 to just above 7. The first wicket can set an innings up with minimal fuss, but we seem to be permanently battling to get off the ground. I am to blame for this at the moment, but it was the same old story last year.

I battled away lethargically for 13 in 90 minutes, before trying to defend a ball in hindsight I could have left. I was actually going to pull away from the ball I was dismissed on: I looked up late in my routine to find the bowler in his delivery stride. Instead I played a hesitant prod and brooded in fury for the rest of the day. We battled our way to 250, perhaps 100 under par. Way too many starts. We have only had one hundred all season, and despite the way the wickets generally have been playing, there should have been no excuses today. Thankfully in fading light, we struck late, with SA teetering at 2–10.

Being out, I did get to see Mike Hussey stroke 81 not out in the Test match – batting with intent, pulling and cutting his way back into form. It was inspirational stuff, back-against-the-wall viewing. Alas, it was too late for me to harness that inspiration.

Saturday, 27 November

Tasmania 251 vs SA 55 (Faulkner 5–5) and 3–91

Today was perhaps the strangest day's play I have been involved in. SA managed just 55 – James Faulkner, a star of the future with his left-arm mediums, taking 5 for 5 with full-length deliveries that just did enough. Bellerive is a very hard place to dominate off the front foot and the visitors paid the price dearly for trying to. We also caught beautifully behind the wicket.

The decision to make them follow on was the correct one, as we had only bowled for 30 overs. The wicket shouldn't deteriorate. They scratched to 90 for the loss of three before the late afternoon rain came. A few early wickets and we could roll through their brittle middle order and record a magnificent victory.

Sunday, 28 November

Tasmania 251 and 5–144 (Bailey 77) vs SA 55 and 416*

Holy shit! How this game can bite you in the arse if you get ahead of yourself. I write this after running home from the ground to clear my head of the despair that engulfed us today. My legs are heavy. My heart too.

The early wickets didn't eventuate and when we finally did get a breakthrough, we were unable to exploit it. We felt like we had Dan Christian plumb LBW second ball. He went on to despatch our undisciplined bowlers to all parts – 90 off 70 balls to leave us chasing 220 instead of 80 or 90. He played bloody well, but we were poor. What should have been a fairly comfortable chase quickly became a nightmare.

I played an absolutely horrendous shot trying to impose myself on the afternoon. A disgracefully undisciplined cover drive to a wide ball, that was by no means a half volley (does this sound like déjà vu – because it bloody well does for me). The moment you realise you have made such a mistake (again) is a very grave one indeed – you feel like you want to crawl into a dark hole with embarrassment, having let yourself and all of your teammates down. You want to throw shit everywhere in rage and disgust. I am not an angry man, but this afternoon it felt like I was. I am angry because I am not learning – making the same mistakes over and over. I am putting so much effort into being better and yet here I am, having let myself down again, writing the same words, having the same thoughts and making the same promises that I did when I played a similar shot against Victoria only four weeks ago.

To make matters worse, we slumped to 4–15 with another contagious collapse. I do feel personally responsible. When fear engulfs a change room, it is like an epidemic that sweeps through with crippling consequences. Panic is cricket's 'silent' killer – no one mentions it; everyone wills it to end; it explodes out of complacency. Perhaps such collapses are worse for arising out of a position of strength – a slight moment of doubt from one, snowballs into collective disbelief; every appeal heightens their excitement; every dismissal furthers our despair.

Thankfully George and James Faulkner counterpunched before James fell late – another bloody 40 from the top order. Starts like this simply shift pressure to the next bloke and compound the problem. We still need 80, but with George still there my money is on us.

The motive for the run home from the ground (8 hilly kilometres) was part punishment for being so disrespectful to my teammates and part cleansing. I thought about my wreck of a season. With half the season gone, I am still to get going, and am miles shy of the goal I had set at the start of the year of batting 25 full sessions; I have managed two. I set myself a revised target: 15 in the next five games. It is a harrowing thing to have to revise goals downward, and it hurt to do so. Today was as low as I've been in years.

My wife Virginia was sitting on the steps waiting for me. Not caring for my sweatiness, she put her arms around me, squeezed so very tightly and simply said, 'I love you regardless of how many runs you get darling – to me there is so much more to you than being a cricketer. Get in the shower and come and have some dinner.' Not a mention of the day followed. I felt blessed, and put further cursing off until tomorrow.

Monday, 29 November

Tasmania 251 and 177 lost to South Australia 55 and 416 by 43 runs

Today was a dark day indeed – perhaps the darkest of my professional career. George was out LBW the very first ball of the day and at no stage did we even put up a fight, losing 5 for 30-odd to whimper to 180 all out. Pathetic. I feel responsible for starting this catastrophe – I think it is only the 18th time in first-class cricket history that a team following on has won. When you play in tight games, often you can feel a sense of belief, an aura surrounding the group, that gets the best out of people in the face of intense pressure. I dared not say it aloud but I could not feel any such presence today. It is hard to describe the silence and disappointment that shrouds a room after a loss like this. Worse still, when a game finishes at close to midday, there is a large part of the day that needs to be filled – a tough proposition when brooding seems the order of the day. Our team has an incredible amount of character – we need to pick ourselves up and do it quickly. Ruts are inevitable in a season but good teams have hiccups, not troughs. I can only pray this is a moment I look back on after a successful season and think 'that made us stronger, hungrier'. Our problem is that none of our batters are making big runs. Usually it comes in waves and spurts. I carry you today, but you will have my back later. All misfiring at once equals disaster. We have not played on a good wicket until this one and the mental scars of seaming balls and sticky footwork were opened when they had no reason to. We need to lift our output individually and drag a mate with us.

In the Test, as though I needed another depression trigger, the English batted and batted and batted. Alastair Cook 200 (I feel a slight sense of happiness born out of respect for his old-fashioned graft) and Jonathan Trott 100 plus. It does show – not that I feel like I need a reminder – sport is not about technique but about willpower, mental discipline and willingness to compete. The more I learn about technique (and I have had my moments of obsessing about it), the more I understand that every technique has holes in it. Slight changes to gain something usually give something away. I came to a conclusion some years ago that everyone is different and whatever works for an individual to conquer the challenges thrust at him, minus a few 'non-negotiables', should be encouraged and not manufactured.

In moments of disillusionment in the last 24 hours, I have questioned writing this diary. Is it making me obsessive, intense and unnaturally analytical? I do feel over-analysis ruins instinct. I rarely watch video of my dismissals. Is writing encouraging all the emotions I want to ignore when I am batting (less describing, more doing)? I will give it another week. Perhaps my motivation to write is just strongly correlated to how many runs I score. And while it feels like a dark week, it could be a hell of a lot darker. Graeme 'Foxy' Fowler wrote a county diary some years ago when he was expecting to be forging his international career, only to lose form, faith in his ability and finally faith in himself. The book describes train wreck after train wreck, eventually including his marriage. The example has been half on my mind as I commit pen to paper every night. I felt ready when I started. Was I? The good thing is that the writing is helping me pull my thoughts together. The bad thing is that it might actually be precipitating those thoughts. I am going to stick with it. While recording the season may be promoting a higher degree of thoughtfulness around failure, it is certainly also acting as a vehicle of renewing hope each night – as though my first step of resurgence from moments of despair is getting it on paper and letting it go. There may be more I need to let go of.

Tuesday, 30 November

'Batting' and scoring runs are two very different practices. I don't like getting suckered into the prior during the season. As a kid I just loved batting. I could not get enough of it. My dad would throw balls at me until it was dark, until he could not lift his arm. 'C'mon, two more good ones' I would say and sometimes shank a few shots on purpose just to get a little bit more time with the pads on.

Now as a late 20-something, I feel in-season volume training can sometimes lack intensity and purpose, willing you into forgetting about trying to improve. But it can be beneficial in other ways, allowing you to just enjoy the moment, the feeling of batting freely without any pressure, rekindling the childhood memories of your love of the game.

Today, volume was what I felt I needed. I just felt like a long, solid hit, which I managed in three sessions in half-hour stints. The last few weeks I have felt stationary at the crease, too still, like a 'rabbit in the headlights' – and a split second behind the play that's left me 2 or 3 centimetres short of where I've needed to be with my feet, and caused me to rush my down swing. It has felt like my bat has been controlling me and not the other way around.

What to do? Perhaps Tim Paine is right. Perhaps I am the 'theory man'. It crossed my mind that introducing a little additional movement might renew my body's interest in batting: I experimented with a little waggle of the bat, just to get it moving. Immediately it felt great. Suddenly I was one step ahead of the ball being flung towards me. Balls started to disappear off the bat with relative ease. I felt in control and hitting shots with more power for less output – as though the bat had become an extension of my own hands. I don't think it was because of the change to white balls, where I have had more success this year, but more to do with the fact that after such a dark couple of days, my motivation to pick myself up (and those around me) was strong.

One advantage of playing so much cricket of late is the little time to ponder or feel too sorry for myself. When playing club cricket many years ago, and trying to make a name, a weekend failure sometimes meant not batting for three or four weeks. Frustrations were drawn out over days and not hours. Now, there always seems another opportunity around the corner to pick yourself up for – and a chance to face your fears.

I received an email today from an old batting colleague, Rodney Davison – my first ever first-grade captain, who did have some first-class success. He wrote 'don't get too far ahead of yourself, get back to basics, playing in the V and batting for time. Hustle singles in front of the wicket and let your strong square of the wicket game come naturally – don't go searching for it under pressure'. Has he been reading my diary?

Wednesday, 1 December
Tasmania 222 (Cowan 62) lost to SA 5–223 (Drew 2–33)

Thursday, 2 December
Our week went from bad to worse. We were timid at the top of the batting order, creeping through our first ten overs.

Although often regarded as the best place to bat, opening the batting in one-day cricket can be very hard work at times – trying to find that balance of attack and resolute defence, risk and reward. Although there are only two men out, which rewards the brave, there are as a result fielders inside the ring, and the premium on singles can bog you down. In this competition, with two new white balls being used, preservation can also be your first instinct. Sometimes you can get yourself into a hole and feel both the change room and scoreboard pressure building, only to play a rash shot and compound the problem by losing a wicket – as we did tonight.

Alex Doolan, who was opening for the first time, got out in the 19th over for an accomplished 40. How often a wicket is falling before the innings break in this competition! Two for 76 at the change of innings seemed defendable when they slumped to 2 for 10, but they fought back to be just 1 ahead at the break. Our fielding was a little off – like the entire team had a head cold. This was our 'thing' and we still couldn't do it.

Our pinch hitter failed to come off in the next power play (I'm yet to see one who has). Surely we are better assigning a batsman the role of being ultra positive. There is more chance that he will not only initially come off, but if he does, he can then reassess and be flexible in his role for the rest of the innings. I think we need to address this. Regardless, we had a productive start to our second innings power play, perhaps our best (37) as Bailey and I asserted ourselves, before George holed out to long-on the first over after it had finished. Travis came and went and then a direct-hit run-out from the deep capped off a middle order collapse. All the time, I had been at the other end, and had found my rhythm and timing, and generally felt a million dollars. It was nice to just be a part of the game again, attempting to control its destiny, having the power to manipulate fields, outfox a bowler, and generally control the pace at which it was being played. I did realise, in among it all, that I was not even trying to watch the ball. Evidently I must have been doing so and closely at that. It was a great reminder of the feeling of complete thoughtlessness that engulfs you when you are playing well.

Every time I was about to launch, though, we lost a wicket, forcing me to abort for another two overs to ensure we did not lose two in such a short space. This happened often enough that I looked up and there were only seven overs to play. This format of the game gets away from you quickly in the later stages. It was great to contribute, but our 220 was unlikely to be enough. We certainly missed Xavier. It was not only his skill and execution of orthodox spin that was visibly absent, but more the fact that our other 'X factor' bowlers like Drew and Krejza often feed off the pressure he builds. Tonight our opponents 'sat on' Jason and Brendan without needing to try anything ambitious.

We need to pick ourselves out of this rut before it turns into an abyss. We play against NSW in Burnie on Saturday, a team chock full of internationals; on our present form, they will blow us away.

Friday, 3 December – Virginia's birthday

Burnie: a quiet industrial seaside town on the north-west coast of Tassie, five hours in a bus for us but a huge trek for the Blues who had come from their last match in Perth – some 15 hours of travel. It is fantastic to get out to regional centres to play. They are usually well attended and there is a general buzz around. What usually lets these kinds of trips down are the facilities, but Burnie is the exception: a superb ground nestled on a point between two beaches. The local council has spent a lot of time and money getting the place up to such a standard.

The wicket looks very wet – it has rained up here all week and will be slow and seamy for the first couple of hours. We trained lightly today. Mist that at times meant you could not see 5 metres in front of you made the town feel like it was a Himalayan village for most of the day. As such, there was no possibility of a net, but we are in the groove and shouldn't need them after two months of solid cricket. The Blues are on a roll; we have hit a speed bump. It's an interesting game in prospect.

Today is my darling wife's birthday. Yet again, due to cricket, I am not present to help her celebrate and shower her with the love and attention she deserves. While I adore what I do, playing a game that I love for a living, there are moments when I crave the normality of the 'outside' world and resent the opportunities that have been taken away. In our first year of dating, I organised a big surprise birthday dinner for her, mostly weighted towards my Sydney friends as Virginia was newish to town. I was called up at the last minute to play for NSW in Melbourne. The party went on, my absence leaving her with a bunch of virtual strangers. I felt sick with embarrassment. It at least gave her a sense what she might be signing up for in the years to come.

Saturday, 4 December

Tasmania 8–189 lost to NSW 3–190 (Cowan 58)

It would have been bloody hard for us to play any worse today. We are currently crippled with fear. When that happens in cricket, the hand tightens on the bat, the feet feel heavy and generally luck goes against you. We were sent in, which did not help us, but we did not help ourselves, looking a little lost at the top. We had meandered to 1–15 off nine when I came in. Had we been playing with confidence, we would have chanced our arm a bit and put a bit of pressure back on the bowlers. Tentative batting makes good bowling seem faultless and allows the bowler to settle in and not have to change a thing.

We then collapsed primarily due to two run-outs, in both of which I was involved, and in one of which I was culpable. There's no worse feeling in cricket than seeing a teammate who trusted you, walk past with betrayal in his eyes. It makes you get that sick, deep feeling of ache and anger in your stomach. Even when it is not your fault, you feel guilty by association. I am not a great partner to run with and it hurts me. Why? I think a lot of the time I am in my own little world, not aware of my partner's presence, and fail to communicate the thoughts in my head quickly enough. Also, I like to create pressure on fielders by taking a few steps down the wicket even if it is a 'no' call just to have active presence at the crease. This adds confusion, but it's a habit I have struggled to get out of in one-day cricket. In cricket, as in life, trust is hard to earn back, and this creates more problems – a self-feeding, run-out causing monster.

Again we were below par with the bat. I stroked 50-odd off too many balls, holding it all together but then getting out trying to launch a little early. Often if you can just hang in an extra over, you can turn your 50 or 60 into an 80 and that can be all the difference. We gave nothing to our bowlers to bowl at, and that awareness sapped our energy in the field.

Streaks are common in sport and although luck plays a part, winning and losing are habit-forming. You hear of teams who find ways to win when they are full of confidence but behind in a game, and vice versa. At this moment we are so worried about making mistakes (something a bad week can bring out in you) that we have lost our greatest asset, which is our flair. The good news is that we are still on top of the table and not playing for another two weeks – hopefully this will allow our nasty rut to be kicked through the natural lapsing of time.

Coach Coyle, who has a great knack of reading the emotions of his team, has given us this coming week off to freshen up – a shrewd move. It would have been easier to call for 'naughty boy training' – an old-school tactic to tackle poor performance, involving early mornings and extra fitness or fielding, where the catches sting and tend to come in rapid fire. These are useless sessions in my mind but one way of trying to ensure that more is given in the next game. The problem with this is that people become not just fearful of failure, but the punishment as well.

I will write tomorrow but then I am tempted to put the pen down for a week as well. My head is telling me I need a break emotionally, while my heart is telling me that doing so would be a cop-out – just because things are not going as planned in four-day cricket, I still need to respect my commitment to finish what I have started with full attention. To not write would be to almost concede that the diary has got the better of me.

Having said that, it is hard to freshen the mind if I am chronicling and analysing what is going on. I'm sure some clarity will come over this time – particularly to my four-day game. I am still undecided whether writing is bogging the mind down or enlivening it. I plan to have a cricket-free week – the garden calls.

Sunday, 5 December

The Aussie Test team are capitulating and Simon Katich is seriously injured. There is no doubt surrounding the fact they will pick Phil Hughes for the next Test, although he has averaged just 16 in first-class cricket this year. I can't complain and doubt I will even be talked about as a prospect by either the press or the selection panel. Often you feel like you are one or two good full seasons away from higher honours. In this case, a couple of scores could have made all the difference.

Monty's one-handed hanger might have changed the course of my career – how many cricketers can claim to have had their destiny shaped by Monty Panesar's fielding?!

Having laid all cricket aside yesterday, I now find myself wishing we had a game. I am committed to finishing the second half of the season strongly – 500 runs and I won't settle for less. This turn of events is perhaps the shot of inspiration I needed.

Tuesday, 7 December

I have been vowing to build some garden beds down the side of the house since the day we moved in over 18 months ago. Blessed with space that we definitely could not have afforded in Sydney and inspired by my love and desire for fresh produce, I had visions of a long and elaborately filled veggie patch. Having never built anything in my life, let alone grown anything, the task at hand had daunted me into inaction. Today was the day that the project finally got some traction. Having searched the foreign landscape of Bunning's for timber, and gotten lost in the seemingly never-ending walls of screws, I ended up with a boot load of materials to make my vision a reality. Almost like a parent bringing home their first born, I had this impending feeling of 'what now?' Realising I was in well over my head, I called the resident team 'chippy' (and opening bowler) Adam Maher to await further instruction. On the promises of chicken sandwiches and a couple of cases of beer, he has promised to come over tomorrow and 'lend a helping hand'. The good thing is that

I haven't thought about cricket at all, despite expecting interludes of musing while driving or doing other things. Perhaps the gardens beds have done the trick already.

Wednesday, 8 December

I am now the proud caretaker of a three-tiered herb garden that has been planted with tiny tomato plants, eggplants, leeks, spring onions, basil, parsley, chillies, spinach and strawberries. For reasons unbeknownst to me, I am filled with a sense of pride and storge towards my new creation. The world of horticulture is new to me. I even googled what should be planted next to what and the benefits of such companion planting.

That is not to say the day was without mishap. I managed to cut straight through a main pipe of the garden's watering system when digging out the lawn to make way for a boxed tier. My first thought: 'My wife is going to bloody kill me'. Thankfully Adam had some landscaper's tape in his ute and the problem was fixed without fuss. It has now occurred to me that Virginia probably won't even find out about what happened until she reads that last sentence.

It was great to spend some time with big 'Mahbo'. He is straightforward, uncomplicated, and generally very grateful for the opportunity of playing professional sport. Four years ago he was struggling with his body and playing third-grade cricket in Sydney. He has now become one of the most reliable bowlers in the country, having remarkably taken a wicket in every innings he has bowled in throughout his shortish career. Most importantly today, I fed off his easygoing nature and found myself lost in the therapy of the fresh air and some manual labour.

Thursday, 9 December

Hobart is a small town. We can see pretty much every suburb from our balcony. The advantages professionally are numerous – stress-free living with no traffic and five minutes to training is certainly one of them. Most importantly proximity allows us to be a close team in more than just the physical sense. As a group, we essentially live in each other's pockets, breathing each other's lives – because we work odd hours, we're our own best company too. In Sydney, your best cricket mate may live over an hour away, making cricket time your only contact and self-reliance an unavoidable outcome. With 'normal' people working 9 until 5, I found there was little company in a big city for a cricketer with a day off. In Hobart, it feels natural to play together because we very nearly live together.

Conversely, you can feel as though you live in a fish bowl. Cricket is the reason for my being here, but in a town with no AFL or NRL presence, there sometimes seems nowhere to hide – the papers or nightly sports report have little else to talk about. Today was one of those days. Looking for a story, the local rag attacked the team's recent performances.

To add to this, Bellerive's oval is clearly visible from where we live – the newly installed light towers a constant reminder of whatever may have happened that day or a provocation for musing when none is called for. Perhaps this is why I have recently found so much solace in Bruny Island – a little slice of paradise just 40 minutes out of town, but with the feeling of being on the other side of the world.

Friday, 10 December

My recent efforts to avoid all things cricket related were put to an end today – I had to play a T20 for my club, Glenorchy. I usually love playing club cricket, I have really enjoyed my time at Glenorchy, even if it has just been hard not having that affection for the club that is born out of it being part of your development (I still think of myself as a Sydney Uni boy and call each Saturday afternoon for a score update). Today, though, it felt wrong to be playing. For one thing, I felt for the young bloke who had been dropped to make room for me in the team. He was probably the guy who goes to every training, no doubt helps with the BBQ on a Saturday, and lives and breathes the success and failure of the Glenorchy Cricket Club. Our next state fixture, too, is a four-day game starting in a week and I did not really see much point in playing in such slapstick. So although I tried hard to get up for it and to be seen to be contributing, I clean missed my third ball and lost my off stump. We play again tomorrow. Even if I do score runs, I am struggling to see the benefit of slogging a couple when it has been my mental discipline not to leave and that has been letting my red ball cricket down. Perhaps it will rain; I find myself hoping for it.

Saturday, 11 December

No rain but perhaps the next best thing – I was dropped down the order to number three and was not required in the run chase. It saved either the embarrassment of another failure or, perhaps worse, getting some runs that will instill bad habits. For much the same reason I don't like playing backyard cricket. I am paranoid that picking up a bat outside of serious fixtures will cause deficiencies to seep into my game. I know this is rubbish, but it's a genuine phobia – I sadly can't delineate anymore the serious and competitive from the jovial and jazz hat. I either want to be at the top of my game to succeed or not play at all.

I managed to have a good chat late this afternoon to a man who has been part-brother, part-mentor – Greg Mail. In my goals for the year I also have a section on my cricketing role models and why they are as such. I simply wrote under Greg's name, 'Mail – never lie down, run machine, professional. Selfless. Passion for the game and his team'.

Greg himself had an interesting career that spanned over ten seasons for NSW. A highly intelligent man, he was regarded as a plodder, and wore it as a badge of honour rather than as a dirty tattoo. When asked by a reporter if his painstaking hundred at the MCG several years ago was the slowest of his career, Greg famously replied: 'You must have never seen me bat before'. He was constantly fighting for his place in the side and constantly had to prove the doubters wrong. I most admired his honesty, integrity and ability to pick himself off the canvas. We spoke today of the importance of patience. Not once this season have I been dismissed by a ball that would have hit the stumps. Greg's parting words were: 'You have all day, mate. What's the rush?'

He was right. I have either been out driving at the ball or perhaps of more concern, defending meekly. If an opening batsman can't defend with confidence, it is fair to assume few runs will flow. I have two options from now on. I can either attack and attempt to get as many as possible before an inevitable mistake or I can keep grinding them out and risk getting knocked over cheaply on sticky wickets – the courage to keep risking the chance of a drawn-out 20 for the satisfaction of a well-constructed 100.

Believe it or not I used to be a bit of a dasher – scoring several hundreds in the first session of grade games in Sydney. Once in a one-dayer I got out in the 36th over for 199 with ten sixes. It seems an eternity ago – almost a different career. Now and again I give glimpses of my old self. Only last season, I scored a hundred in a session, although it was the second hundred of my innings. Why the evolution? It is partly because the game now means so much more to me. At 20, the world's your oyster, you are fearless and have not been scarred by failure. You are not playing for your career (or, you may be but can't see it at the time). Nor is the game your living. Those days were littered with entertaining innings, but never consistency.

Growing up, my father, rather risk averse himself, would monotonously tell me the old adage, 'Don't push the world along and live in a world of fame, be like the Oxen and get there just the same'. It's what I did. I vowed to give nothing away, to make every innings count in my favour.

Interestingly, I was told at the start of this season by a senior person at Cricket Australia that if I wanted to play Test cricket, I needed to score at a quicker clip. I replied that the last time I checked, Test cricket was played over five days. But perhaps subconsciously this has played on my mind. The wickets have simply not been conducive to attacking batting displays – 'getting in' has been hard enough. Yet maybe I've been batting for other people rather than myself and my team. Surely I am too old for that – if I am going to fall on a sword, it may as well be on my own terms.

Cricket, with all its oddity of technique and styles, is one of the few sports where selectors play the role of God. They above all else have a right to veto your dreams. I have always played my best cricket when playing the situation that presents itself and not concerning myself with others who aren't teammates. It now seems clear that the only way forward is to scrape and fight, all the while batting with positive intent. If I am going to leave, I am going to do so with conviction. If I defend, I am going to do it on my terms. If they are going to get me out, they better be bowling at the stumps.

Sunday, 12 December

My new favourite event in Hobart takes place in a parking lot on a Sunday morning. The farmers' market, which until yesterday I did not know even existed, is foodie heaven. You walk in to see local producers proudly selling their goodness to the world. The star of the show is undoubtedly Matt Evans of *Gourmet Farmer* TV fame – I was even too nervous to go and ask for a photo. After a few (too many) glasses of wine at dinner last night, the freshly laid egg and honey-cured bacon roll (just baked) certainly hit the spot.

I spent the rest of the day with my wife planting trees in our backyard. I had visions of golf, but thought better of it. There is so little family time at this time of year that the last thing I should be doing is running away from it. It was a concession I was happy to make, considering that Virginia does so on a daily basis. Our backyard is on a rock shelf, so it is fair to say she got her value for money on the labour front. Even the worst days of cricket are better than digging ditches.

Tuesday, 14 December

We came together for the first time as a group in over a week in preparation for this Friday's four-day fixture. While I enjoyed the time away, I loved being back in among it – hearing the gossip, soaking up the banter. It looks as though Jon Wells will be dropped for this game and Cossie will move up to open the innings. While our bowlers have taken 20 wickets in each game so far, it is our batting that continues to let us down. We also have the added luxury of Xavier being back from the Test team. He will be disappointed he did not do better given the opportunity, but he was not helped by the fact he was continually bowling to players that were set in their innings.

Our attack is quickly becoming the most disciplined in the country. It will never blow teams away with raw pace or aggression, but each bowler provides something different, and all have the ability to move the ball with skill and precision. They tend to pitch the ball up, are incredibly patient and have a pack mentality. There has been no let up for the opposition – their line has importantly made batsmen, not used to the seamy conditions, play at the ball. Their constant wickets have kept us in every fixture. If we are to give this competition a shake, it is our collective batting efforts that need to be improved – we only have one hundred between us, and have been relying heavily on Mark Cosgrove's resilience, Alex Doolan's starts and lower order rallies. I am among those to blame. Still, I trained today with great energy and enthusiasm. The dark times of ten days ago seem an eternity away.

Friday, 17 December

WA 108 (Faulkner 3–15) vs Tasmania 1–146
(Cosgrove 90*, Cowan 0)

We won the toss and bowled today on the best-looking wicket of the year, and by lunch we found ourselves batting – extraordinary scenes unfolded all morning. We were good with the ball without being exceptional. They looked untroubled for their first 30 runs, before a run-out, as they often do, caused a momentous collapse. Jim Faulkner, backing up his 5–5 in our last fixture, repeated the dose with a probing spell that saw WA lose 8–30. It all happened so very quickly, it made it all quite hard to fathom. A last wicket slog pushed them past three figures.

Our batting has been brittle, but today showed excellent resolve. Mark Cosgrove has so far played superbly – his deft touches of late cuts are of a bygone era. Dools also played straight and in his bubble. Prior to the game we talked about the batters doing less talking and more batting and by the time the rain came we were 50 ahead for the loss of only my wicket.

Some days are just not meant to be (I seem to say that a lot …). Bizarrely, a butterfly flew across my helmet a split second before the release of the ball. I should have pulled out; instead, I played the line of Hogan's first ball that nipped across me, and nicked it to first slip for a duck. A butterfly: it's got to be the ultimate soft dismissal. Had I been in great form, I doubt I'd even have noticed it.

I am sitting here willing myself to keep the faith; to keep it simple, to keep trusting my instinct and preparation and it will turn for me. Today was another day that I had pumped myself up for, only for the balloon of expectation to self deflate. If I don't keep the faith from here, it will all start to eat me up inside and the battle will be lost before it even starts. I feel a little empty personally, but pleased that we are in such good shape. I just received a call from Dan Marsh – a friend and mentor to many in our team. He simply asked, 'How are you going?' That's cricketer speak for 'How fragile are you feeling and do you want to talk about it?' I told him I was okay but frustrated. He offered that, more than ever, now was not the time to start doubting myself – just to keep everything simple. When you score a hundred, your phone runs hot. When you get a duck, you only hear from those who really care, and even they sometimes feel as though they should stay at arm's length.

NSW has jumped the field, and we, despite playing unpredictably and patchily, have found ourselves in equal second with a team that has played one more game than us. A win here could well and truly set us up for the home stretch. After this game, we don't play another first-class game for seven weeks as the Big Bash kicks in, only highlighting how important the next three days are, not only for the team, but also for myself.

Saturday, 18 December

AM: I tossed and turned all night, my little brain fuelled by frustration and I was unable to rest. Why am I wasting good form? I have just scored back-to-back fifties in one-day cricket and feel at the top of my game. If you don't know where your next run is coming from, you may be shrouded in self-doubt, but burning frustration is not an emotion you have to deal with. To get out of this little red ball trough I have found myself in (13, 0, 0 and one fifty in eight innings) I have to trust my preparation, be consistent in doing it, and just be willing and able to meet each day's opportunities and challenges with vigour and sharpness. All that counts is today – I can't waste mental energy on the past.

PM: *Tasmania 258 (Cosgrove 100, Doolan 51) vs WA 108 and 4–220*

We still have our noses in front in the context of the game, but we did ourselves no favours, again collapsing, losing nine wickets within the first session. Cossie brought up his second hundred of the year and then lost his leg stump moments later. Dools slashed at one and this being such a hard wicket to start on, the middle order came and went quickly. It is often feast or famine at Bellerive. I once played there for NSW in a game where no fewer than 12 ducks were spread over both teams. We certainly had our chance to nail them but we let it severely slip. Thankfully our last wicket put on over 50 runs in six overs of streaky hitting, to completely change the complexion of our innings. James Faulkner, coming in at six, showed his batting talents to finish with 50-odd not out. I think he is going to be a brilliant bowling all-rounder, someone who can bat at seven (for us and Australia) and bowl first change. For such a youthful cricketer, he has the cricket smarts – a skill perhaps hardest to learn.

A lead of 150 is significant regardless of conditions but they fought back well in a gripping afternoon's cricket. Just as they had clawed back into the contest, we ran out Shaun Marsh brilliantly and then Marcus North received a rough LBW decision (when your luck runs out, it really runs out). Our tight bowling and fantastic energetic bubble in the field then slowly asphyxiated their middle order. There are four overs in the morning before the second new ball and the first hour could well determine the outcome of the game.

Sunday, 19 December

*WA 108 and 255 (Butterworth 4–59) lost to Tasmania 258
and 0–106 (Cosgrove 86*) by 10 wickets*

Rarely do things fall into place so perfectly. A wicket in the first over of the new ball was followed by a brilliant direct-hit run-out to dismiss Adam Voges – Butterworth dived full length and threw the stumps down from his knees at a deep gully. WA's last six added just 30.

Mark Cosgrove then dismantled their attack with 86 off 50 balls to ensure there were no chasing jitters and a repeat of our last game – the game was done and dusted before lunch (on day three!). Cossie has a fierce dose of self-belief. He'd had a run-in on the first day with Michael Beer, whose confidence had evidently been enhanced from his recent Test call up. Today he made a point of taking Beer down, smashing him everywhere. Each time Beer became more verbally aggressive, Cos responded with another boundary; every time he crossed the bowler's path, he growled, 'You really are quite shit, aren't you?' When the bowler at one stage quipped that Cossie was carrying some excess weight, Cossie dispatched the next one, with the follow-up: 'Mate, I don't need to run when you're bowling!' There are few who can back up their words with such destructive actions. As for me, I got the best seat in the house and was happy to quietly accumulate a 20 not out. An hour of batting that just triggered how it feels to be in a four-day contest with the bat. We moved to second place on the ladder but now won't play again for another six weeks.

Monday, 20 December

Instead of taking the unused last day of the WA game as a day off, we used the time as a bonus and topped up our one-day and T20 batting skills. I don't think I'll play much part in the Big Bash competition, which disappoints me, particularly as I have been our most consistent one-day player this season. It's just that our research suggests that the team hitting most boundaries tends to win in T20, and it's not thought I hit enough.

I am disappointed for several reasons – firstly, I think I can do the job and may well surprise a few people. I am a big believer in picking your best six batsmen and trusting them to succeed in any format. Secondly, there is more than one way to skin a cat – you don't have to be a big hitter to get the ball to the fence (as I have proven in the one-day comp). I'm a little disillusioned that they will pick guys on 'six-hitting' potential and leave out someone who knows how to score runs.

We play our next fixture – a one-day game against WA – on Wednesday night. It is a great chance for us to get our limited overs season back on track.

Wednesday, 22 December

WA 6–245 (Doherty 2–46) lost to Tasmania 6–246 (Cowan 82, Bailey 79*) by 4 wickets

We were back to our best today, the Tigers of old, playing fearless, aggressive and confident one-day cricket. Our opponents were slightly off their game in the field and failed to match our intensity and presence. Xavier opened the bowling and WA failed to take any initiative against him, and found themselves behind for the rest of the game. On the best wicket we've seen this year, we made short work of their 84 before our break. Marcus North, who got me out three times in three innings last season, immediately brought himself on when I got to the crease. My plan, which I had worked on tirelessly yesterday, was to hang back in my crease and try to hurt him either side of point. It worked and allowed me to rotate the strike at will.

Despite some late-order hitting, their 245 was never going to be enough on such a good wicket. They squandered a few starts and we were good in the field, but they generally played as though they were waiting for us to make the mistakes. George and I took the game away from them by putting on 130 for the third wicket. My 82 at better than a run-a-ball was as well as I have ever played in one-day cricket. There were moments when I felt I could hit the ball anywhere I liked. As the bowler ran in, I said to myself a few times 'this is going'. There is certainly no better feeling than being the guy controlling the team's destiny and changing the pace of the game simply because it is 'your night' – for that moment, you are in such control of your skill, you can. There is no emotion in such moments; it feels as though you are not even watching the ball as it comes down, and reacting as though you knew all along what was going to be bowled. After I managed to slog one into the stands (a rare occurrence) I cheekily asked George mid pitch if that still would have been 6 in T20. Maybe I had been out to prove a point all night.

Thursday, 23 December

With such a packed schedule pre Christmas (six four-day and eight one-day games) we have not had a moment to even contemplate the fast-approaching T20 season. Despite last night's late finish, and with little sleep, we committed ourselves to playing out a few T20 scenarios in the middle this morning, and despite the arctic lashings blowing up the river, we completed an upbeat session. It was a chance to do, and then immediately evaluate; talking through general tactics and how we could do things differently. I do believe that the shorter the game, the more that chunks of it can be pre-planned. It was essentially a three-hour team meeting, with the field acting as the whiteboard.

I had a bat, and could hardly move after last night – crippled with tiredness of both the mind and body. It felt as though I was in a bat-off of sorts. I would be disappointed if not making any runs at half 8 in the morning, having just batted the team to victory less than 12 hours earlier on the same patch of grass, was deciding my fate for the coming weeks.

Friday, 24 December

Two more sleeps until Boxing Day. Christmas to many Australians is simply a means of providing fresh ham off the bone for the Boxing Day Test match. Our initial plan was to go back to Sydney for Christmas, but we were told months ago that we would be training over the festive period and so had resigned ourselves to a Hobart Christmas – my first without my family. As it turned out, the Tigers' schedule was changed two weeks ago and by then, we were unable to get a flight off the island. I was a little peeved at my life again being so heavily dictated by my cricketing schedule. Instead, I took Virginia to Bruny Island for the first real summer's day we have had, and indulged ourselves in locally produced cheese and oysters, and beaches – a great way to escape the cricket scene and finally relax – something that would have been impossible to do in the hustle and bustle of Sydney.

Saturday, 25 December – Christmas Day

I went for a long run today. It is a bit of a Christmas tradition – do some training when others are indulging in Christmas pudding. It is nice to know you are probably the only one slugging it out – sportsmen are a weird bunch; they will do anything for a mental edge on opponents.

We enjoyed a wonderful Christmas afternoon at the home of Ali and Anna DeWinter. Along with our neighbours and the rest of the Tigers' community, they have become a part of our Tasmanian family and made us feel right at home.

Sunday, 26 December

Boxing Day – where else would I be but in front of a TV? I went to a day of the last Ashes Boxing Day Test. Shane Warne took his 700th Test wicket in my presence. Never have I heard noise like it – the MCG momentarily turned into Albert Park at Grand Prix time. The cricket tragic that I am, I have just watched a YouTube clip to relive the moment and welled up with tears. Recently, the occasion has brought out the best in the greats of the game. Looking up at the honour board in the change room when last playing at the G, I saw five ML Haydens and four RT Pontings in gold. That probably tells you all you need to know.

As I write, Australia have been dismissed for 98. What is this? For much of my living memory, Boxing Day has been an occasion on which the national team has put their opponents to the sword, and in doing so, reassured the entire nation that the game is in good hands, including those who might only watch one day of cricket a year. The Ashes will now not be won. Perhaps it would have been different had England batted first. I know there'll be some hard-nosed men in that Australian dressing room who will be hurting and feeling like they have let themselves and their country down – and I do think the public are wrong when they sometimes insinuate otherwise. I turned the train wreck off at tea time, wondering if I had just witnessed a 'where were you when' moment. There could be some interesting repercussions from today's events.

Monday, 27 December

While the disaster of the Test match was unfolding, Tim Paine passed his fitness test on his finger, recovering incredibly quickly from his finger operation. This has the flow-on effect of me not being selected for the first T20 team to Perth.

His finger is still the size of a Hungarian sausage. I have

been throwing him balls in the nets, and watching him catch with tremendous pain. When he was operated on, the surgeon thought it would be at least a two-month recovery. So far it has been a tick over five weeks. He is a bloody tough character, and proved last year he is perhaps the most valuable player in the competition. So while his return is bad news for me, it is excellent news for the Tigers. I had privately backed him to not have been available for at least another week, but it seems he is determined to get back to playing as soon as possible. Stu Clark told me after my nasty foot injury, 'When you think you are ready, wait another ten days'. He was proved correct. I played, but was barely functional. But I know Tim is keen to prove his fitness as quickly as possible with World Cup selections looming so I can hardly blame him.

Interestingly, Painey too suffered from the stigma of being a plodder – like me at the moment. A few years ago, Tassie could not find a T20 spot for him. How he has broken that mould. Last year he hit more sixes than anyone in the competition and that has given me great inspiration. He found his role at the top of the order, backed his ability and has flourished into a formidable T20 player. Sadly, we would attempt to play much the same role in a game of T20 and there is no room for both of us – in the captain's mind, you can really only afford to have one guy attempting to bat through the innings.

On the other hand, I only feel disappointment as a professional. I have made my case to the best of my ability, and I'll continue trying to make it. NSW was a hard, sometimes bitter, selection experience; I have a lot of faith in the people and processes in Tasmania. So much so, that I want to be the biggest part I can be in their success.

Tuesday, 28 December

I did my best today not to show my disappointment of non-selection and felt all the better for it, even if I was probably a little lacking in intensity. When you know you are not playing, a feeling of flatness is probably inevitable. I couldn't help but watch the hitting of Cosgrove, Birt and Bailey. It was awesome. Perhaps I am indeed a long way off where I need to be.

I am now going to go to Sydney for four days to catch up with family and attend a good friend's wedding – an opportunity very rarely afforded during the cricket season. Hopefully it will be a tonic – a silver lining of sorts. But if I don't manage to play any T20 cricket, it may be a very slow month. From here, the season slips away quickly.

Wednesday, 29 December

Oddly, I found out today that I have made the final 350 players for the IPL auction. 'Entry forms' were emailed out a few weeks ago and I imagine every domestic player in the country would have returned theirs promptly. It has quickly become the shortest route to cricket riches in this country, and I put my name up more as a bit of a joke, viewing it as a lottery – you have to be in it to win it. There is probably more chance of me flying to the moon than being picked up by any of the

IPL franchises, but with our entire one-day domestic cricket season now beamed into India, you just never know your luck. I do think it would be fun to go over – for India rather than for the 'Mickey Mouse' cricket. When NSW toured there in 2006, Greg Mail and myself flash-packed around for an additional two weeks after the others had gone home. We had the experience of a lifetime. It was incredible to get among the sights, tastes, smells and sounds as everyday tourists rather than touring cricketers.

As well as everything and everywhere else, the IPL has fundamentally altered the economics of domestic cricket in this country. In the pre-IPL world, there were only ever about 25 meaningful livings to be made by cricketers in this country – those offered Cricket Australia contracts. The only way to achieve that prosperity was to represent your country, and you devoted your whole being to that end. Cricket Australia benefited richly from that accumulated effort, and the absence of competition from other potential employers. The IPL has spread the wealth, and significantly enhanced expectations of how much money can be made from cricket – an important consideration for talented teens who might be making up their minds about the relative attractiveness of various sporting options.

It has also meant that you can be paid a lot more for not being as good as you used to have to be. Perhaps that's more 'democratic', but it also seems to make efficiency sufficient when the objective should surely always be excellence. If the game is to remain healthy in this country, our local system has to be centred around producing players whose lasting goal is to play for the country. To me, T20 pays too much for certain quite limited skills – although perhaps I feel that more acutely than most because (at the moment anyway) I am still trying to cultivate them!

Thursday, 30 December

Sitting back and watching the team you usually play for on television is a strange experience. You notice nuances of the team's play that you perhaps usually wouldn't. We were white hot, fielded terrifically and cruised to victory on the back of some excellent Birt and Paine hitting.

It was very entertaining from the comfort of the couch, until it was over anyway, when I really missed being a part of the celebration – singing the team song huddled tightly in a circle, arms around shoulders, seeing the joy in the eyes of your teammates. My feelings have not changed as to my involvement or lack thereof – the more I watch, the more convinced I am that I could contribute anywhere from one to six.

Sunday, 2 January 2011

A lot has been written about Australian cricket in the midst of the Ashes drubbing that is currently being handed out. Some have looked at the shape that domestic cricket is in – which is interesting given that many of those opining about it would not have been near domestic cricket for some time, if at all.

When I started out for NSW, Shield cricket was indeed

very strong and extremely competitive. Queensland had the likes of Maher, Love, Bichel, Seccombe and Michael Kasprowicz; Lehmann, Blewett and Gillespie turned out for SA. There were no easy games. Each team had at least one player who was world class and would have proved it at international level had he had the opportunity. The difference now is not in the first-choices XIs – they are still strong. What is noticeable is that the quality falls away among replacements, in the bottom 20 per cent of Shield squads. I don't always agree with the cliché that you are only as good as your worst player, but I do think it is relevant in this regard.

Five years ago, Cricket Australia decided to advance younger players more quickly, by replacing the traditional second XI competition, where each state would invariably pick their next best team, with an Under 23s competition (with an allowance of three over-age players). Apologists argued that it was necessary to sweep away players who were 'clogging up the system', having reached their late 20s without maturing into internationals, in favour of a younger brigade who potentially could. Players at the time could not comprehend this move. All of a sudden accomplished players in the larger states (I am talking from a NSW perspective) were merely treading water if they found themselves out of favour or form, relegated to playing club cricket that they had dominated for six, seven or eight years already. In their place, talented but not yet ripe youngsters, not quite across the game as a whole, let alone their own, were given preferences for places. It has taken a few years but we are now reaping what we sowed as a cricket community.

Because those fringe players (some had played more than 50 first-class games) are no longer in the system, the gap between the best domestic players and the worst has widened dramatically. My memories of second XI cricket are littered with older, hard-nosed professionals vying for places in the top team. It was sometimes tougher to score runs in those games than in first-class cricket – the wickets were certainly more bowler-friendly and playing 12 allowed an extra bowler to be picked, allowing them to rest and be fresh for their next short burst. In a game of note, the Victorian attack featured Nannes, Harwood, Darren Pattinson, Denton, Siddle and McDonald, all well over the age restrictions now in place, and all played international cricket within 12 months. Nathan Bracken got plucked from our team in the same week and was flown to the sub-continent for the international series that was being played. It was a tough initiation ceremony for any youngster who was deemed good enough to have earned their spot – if they succeeded they were indeed ready to contribute to the first team. It also gave them an opportunity to learn from those who were far more experienced – how they prepared, how they dealt with pressure and how they survived in the then jungle of professional cricket. Competition bred hunger – hunger that filtered right up through the ranks. Sadly this is now long gone – the U/23 experiment in my mind is the single biggest error of judgment that has been made in the administration of the game in recent years.

Gideon Haigh mused in *The Australian* (among other things) that the now T20-centric system was partly to blame.

I tend to agree. While I am no behavioural finance expert, one of the first things they taught us at university was that humans react to incentives – and this format is the most lucrative and prestigious in town. Less work for more play – why would someone of David Warner's ilk hone his skills for the physical toil of first-class cricket when for him, there is no incentive to?

In a rare bright spot, Usman Khawaja has been selected for his Test debut. He will undoubtedly acquit himself with calm and grace. What can I add to the Usman story that is not currently being reported in every major news source? He is an intelligent young man whose Asian politeness is seasoned with Australian self-deprecation and humour. When he finished his studies and was granted his pilot's licence, he urged his teammates not to annoy him – 'A Muslim who can fly planes is a dangerous combination'. He makes the game look simple, uncomplicated and enjoyable. He is one of the NSW players that I felt like I had a bond with away from cricket, but one I also loved talking cricket with. We opened the batting a lot together over the years, and like few partnerships, clicked from the very first mid-pitch chat.

In his famous tell-all diary of the 1969 baseball season, Jim Bouton described the three types of athletes that exist. The first is 'a guy who does everything instinctively and does it right in the first place'. The second 'have the tools but are always too involved with the mechanics'. There is a third, which is Usman to a tee: 'the one who is intelligent enough to know that [baseball] is basically an instinctive game'.

Monday, 3 January

Today was an excellent reminder of the plight of a struggling professional cricketer – when you are out of the team, you might as well not exist. You bat when bowlers have finished their work, satisfy your own needs and move on. Frankly, it didn't do me any harm. It was a good reminder to look after those on the outside when I am back on the inside. You can be too absorbed in yourself sometimes, such are the battles of the mind in this game. You need to remind yourself to relax and enjoy the ride, and try and make it as enjoyable for your mates around you as well.

Tuesday, 4 January

Finally, a full-blown T20 practice game! It is hard to break into any team, or improve for that matter, when there is no opportunity to do so. The current first team batters took on the bowlers with the gaps being filled by the rest of us. Surprisingly to them, but not to us (the bowlers) we won a fairly lame game of cricket. Chasing 101 we snuck home on the back of some clever batting from Alex Doolan – another on the T20 periphery who knows how to score runs. I was determined to be ultra aggressive, and ended up with a solid 21 off fewer balls on a wicket not conducive to stroke play. Often the difference in the shorter forms is how many well-struck shots pick out fielders, and I was a little disappointed not to have 30-odd off 20 as I might have, but I felt confident enough afterwards to email George about my T20 role, and about where he felt I needed to improve.

GB

I wanted to have a chat this coming week about T20 cricket, so thought I could give you a heads up, so you can have a think prior to this. It was fascinating watching the other night from the other side of the fence. I thought we were white hot. I want to be a part of a team that will no doubt give it a shake. I missed singing the song and seeing the happiness in the guys' eyes.

We obviously have very differing views in regards to what I can offer the team, which is fine, I am just frustrated by the lack of opportunity to prove you otherwise. Every time you have asked me to improve something (eg scoring quicker in ODs), I feel I have found a way to do it, but I now can't get any better at T20 just by watching it.

I don't want the next month to just meander along if I am not going to be in the team, so I just want some guidance as to where you think I need to improve my T20 skills so I can go away and work on them.

Regardless of opportunity, I want to be improving. So if you could take 5 mins to have a think about this, it would be fab GB and very much appreciated.

With support as always
EC

It helps to put things in writing – thus this diary, I guess. I want him to know that I am keen to contribute to the T20 campaign. I want to be in his calculations. I wouldn't do this with just any captain. I certainly would never have done it in NSW. But it's really a mark of my respect for George and the culture of honesty and fair dealing he's helped build in Tasmania, that I'm prepared to put myself forward in this way.

Wednesday, 5 January

> Cook has a rare sense of ease at the crease. He does not so much concentrate as absorb himself in his activity – his batting lacks strain and complication and is all straight levers and sweet swings. Simplicity counts among his assets – staying within his limitations. Decades ago, it was said to the Duke of Wellington that he was remarkable, not for the extent of his abilities, but the use he made of those he possessed. Cook is the same, he does not step down the pitch or sweep or seldom troubles the covers. Rather, he cuts, clips, tucks and glides and bats a very long, long time.
>
> —Peter Roebuck,
> *Sydney Morning Herald*

It is fair to say that Alastair Cook has inspired me this summer – to be myself, to keep it simple and to be the one to win matches as an old-fashioned opener. I hope to take this inspiration and make it work for me come early February when the first-class season resumes.

I do acknowledge the irony of looking to an Englishman (perennially Australian cricket prey) for inspiration and a reiteration of the game's blessed basics. Apart from the reincarnated Mike Hussey, role models from our side of the fence have not been particularly thick on the ground this summer

– we look to be subsiding again in Sydney, with a 3–1 score line around the corner.

Thursday, 6 January

George has responded to my email:

> Read your email after our quick chat in the gym the other day, which probably didn't offer you much you didn't know.
>
> Have had a think about it and have come up with these thoughts – some you may agree with some not, but as always happy to chat to you more if you desire.
>
> 1. I think you could play T20 as the player you are. That player is best suited to having explosive players around him.
>
> 2. However, sometimes I feel when you are surrounded by those players or given the 'bloke to bat around' role your mindset can become a little defensive. Your best short form cricket I have seen is when you are attacking. Particularly when your intent is to rotate the strike from ball 1 and to look to change if a bowler is bowling well.
>
> 3. One area I think you can improve is your power hitting. Not necessarily new shots but knowing that if you get a ball in your zones you can clear the pickets with it. I think you do this well square of the wicket – down the ground is an area I think you could improve as is when it is a spinner or medium – you do enjoy the pace of the ball coming on.

4. Lastly: this is probably the point of most conjecture, is just to have as much dynamism in your game as possible. The 7 batters we have in our 13 at present, I feel, can all win a game from their own bat in a short period. I feel you would have to bat most of the innings to have that impact. If we need a six NOW can you deliver?

This can be argued both ways. Having that person to bat around can work perfectly – but for this campaign, as a first option, we went down the other path of going for our most dynamic, destructive batters and hoping they come off.

As I said in the gym, I think you can play t20 just fine – and with Paine a sure thing for WC team + Xavier probably going as well – you may well get a chance this tournament. And it will be right at the big game time.

As with all batting the biggest thing to have is clarity of your role and what you can do. For your game I would be working hard on nailing the boundary shots you already have and in between those be working on striking the ball cleanly and hard into gaps and running those Teddy legs off. These are both things that I have seen you working on so I think you have the right idea.

Will ring tomorrow as I have a lucky moment in life story for you.

Night
GB

George's response was everything that encapsulates him as a man and captain – it was fair-minded, thoughtful, and compassionate but managed to be firm and did not offer false hope. Above all, it was honest; as a player, I know I appreciate that more than anything else.

Friday, 7 January

I am writing this while watching the Tigers get absolutely thumped at The Gabba. It hurts most as I know that deep down I could be adding value to the team – with the bat, in the field, helping settle the nerves. It is tough to digest. When I have been left out of sides in the past, there has always been a sense of schadenfreude, but that is certainly not the case tonight.

In comparison to watching the team win last week, where there was a painful sense of longing to be a part of the excitement, tonight the pain was caused by shaking my head in disbelief at our ability to play so poorly. I think that it is exacerbated by the format – T20 has a knack of making good players look like hacks, and the skilful look inept.

Saturday, 8 January

A rare appearance in grade cricket yielded some much desired time at the crease with a brisk and controlled hundred. Playing club cricket has certainly varied in importance over the years. When it is where you play most of your cricket, there is a sense of huge importance to the occasion – and so there should be; you are playing at the level that is still required to be conquered. When you progress, it becomes about keeping your game ticking over. I still care if we win and I still care for making runs. Perhaps my biggest fear as a cricketer is being known as the guy who 'does not try in club cricket'. Even when playing overseas, I have ensured a level of professionalism in my approach to my game. I feel as though you owe it to the club for whom who are a member, and more importantly to the guy who has been dropped for you to play. I also kind of like being the big fish for a day – answering all the 'what is it like' questions with unusual enthusiasm.

It felt today as though I was as technically efficient and as mentally zoned as I have been for some time. Like I have been in one-day cricket, my hands felt relaxed and in sync with the pace of the ball coming at me. It can often be tough coming back to grade cricket but today I was really focused on finding the balance of occupying the crease and batting time while being really physically and mentally positive. I hit it hard and straight and felt a million dollars. At times I felt like I was on auto-pilot, bullying the ball around on a low slow wicket, not thinking or over-complicating. Club cricket is far removed from first-class cricket but any reminder of playing well is always welcome. As they say, regardless of the level, you've still got to get them.

Monday, 10 January

I think I need some time out. I find myself watching every T20 game that is live on television (most nights), analysing (and enjoying) – trying to get a feel for the game and what is required with the bat in different roles. I'm going a little crazy with frustration and maybe even, if I am honest, some resentment.

I am familiar with this feeling from my years in NSW. A professional sportsman 'is' his performances. When you are not performing, it can feel as though you have ceased to exist. I am luckier than most. I have a degree, and have worked in roles far removed from cricket. But no wonder cricketers are inclined to stave off retirement. Life without the game is the great unknown, where there is no avoiding the question: 'Who am I really?'

In my last season in NSW, when my pickings were really slim, and I had too much time on my hands, I decided to allocate some of it to working as a volunteer in a homeless shelter. Looking back, I was probably more broken than I let on to others. So totally was I invested in the idea of making cricket my living that when there was no cricket, there could almost be no living either: with that attitude, in hindsight, I was bound to fail. My time in the shelter helped cure me of that. There was less time to worry and, I soon saw, far less to worry about. I liked the work. I liked the people. The life was real – I could see the artificiality of my own self-created dilemmas. Runs became less meaningful – with the result I started scoring them heavily again.

I like to think that having had this experience, I am more objective about my cricket now. So why is my omission from the Tiger's T20 team bugging me so? Perhaps it is professionalism. When there is no cricket, I have next to nothing to do, unless I make it for myself. Perhaps success starves you of your capacity to amuse yourself and leads to undirected, potentially destructive thoughts; maybe we disserved ourselves when we made first-class cricket a full-time occupation. It left us with nothing to focus on but a finite number of places, with a yawning gulf between the experiences of being the 11th best player and the 12th. They are feelings I need to rise above.

Tuesday, 11 January

With rain in the air, I was asked to join the T20 group for the game tonight against Victoria, with the theory being that a shorter game will require more batsmen. Having decanted some of my negative thoughts into this diary, I actually felt good, happy to be around the team again, but not feeling as though my whole life hinged on the experience.

In the end, I did not play, and the team were superb – the gap between our best and worst in this format in this game is immense. Tasmania won by nine wickets, and Jon Wells played brilliantly with a freedom that I had not seen from him for some time. Despite competing for the same spot, I was genuinely happy to see him do so well.

Friday, 14 January

I was given some advice from a very successful cricket journalist and author when I mentioned this writing project to him. He said, if it is boring to write, it will surely be boring to read. Heeding this, I have avoided writing for the last couple of days.

Saturday, 15 January

Almost humorously, grade cricket was called off last night due to the volume of rain this week. Today was perfectly still, sunny and 25 degrees – a cricketer's nirvana. There could well be some sore heads in club land today.

Sunday, 16 January

Slow weeks in Hobart mean I get to read. It seems any non-fiction I pick up at the moment has me contemplating the book's relevance to cricket. Michael Lewis' *Moneyball* had me convinced the Oakland Athletics were the Tassie Tigers in disguise – a team making a very efficient use of their often-scant resources. When I suggested this to a friend with an interest in economics, he retorted that too many resources breed waste. It made me think of my time in NSW and how many good players had either slipped through their net or simply went to waste on the sidelines.

It also (as previously mentioned) had me thinking that cricket's go-to statistics are archaic and often give a false impression of a player's importance and contribution. Why don't we measure the percentage of dot balls a batsman faces in OD cricket when rotating the strike is considered the most important skill of middle-order batting? Strike rate gives such a narrow view of such issues. If someone hits every eighth ball for 6, but does not score off the other seven, is he doing a good job? I would suggest not – the pressure on his partner to score in between these boundaries would be immense. Why do we have a runs-per-over evaluation for bowlers, when the only important issue is whether they are bowling at below the current required rate. If someone is going at 8 an over, typically you would think he has had a poor day, but if the required rate is 15, I would suggest he is actually winning the game for his team. The statistics cricket relies on so heavily rarely tell the full story. I have already used the example earlier in the diary of averages and hundreds. I am sure there are many more that don't come to mind off the top of my head.

Nassim Taleb's *The Black Swan* stimulated many a thought on the role of randomness in sport. A black swan in cricket is an unexpected event that changes the direction of a game or a career. The one moment that keeps coming back to me was Shoaib Akhtar having Justin Langer plum LBW first ball in Peshawar, only to have Steve Bucknor turn down the appeal for reasons unknown to anyone but him. Here was a man who gave cricket everything. If desire and diligence were runs, Langer would have out-averaged Bradman. But everything – his career, his future, his life – ended up hinging on someone else's split-second, and probably inaccurate, judgment. With the reprieve, he grafted a hundred and rebuilt his reputation, played a hundred Tests and recently became Australia's batting coach. When I was growing up the clichéd adage 'the harder you work the luckier you get' sounded like gospel. Having read *The Black Swan*, I realise it should have read, 'the harder I work, the more prepared I am to take advantage of serendipitous events'.

Malcolm Gladwell's argument in *Blink* is that spontaneous decisions are often better than those carefully planned – avoiding confusion and distraction from a surfeit of information. To me, the book just reaffirmed all of my beliefs on batting. Training hones the subconscious' ability to deal with all the information – ball trajectory, speed and variability of bounce – then the best way of performing under pressure is to try and tap into this honed instinct, avoiding paralysis by analysis, as Gladwell puts it. I've written in this diary about the 'zone' of concentration, a feeling of not forcefully and consciously watching the ball – rather letting the subconscious pick up cues from the bowler's actions and reacting accordingly. So Gladwell's thesis certainly struck a chord with me. His reference to a fireman entering a building and intuitively knowing where the source of the fire is (based on noise and heat) reminded me of what good batting feels like.

Monday, 17 January

Such is the (financial) importance of T20 for the states, we generally travel to games with 13 players. We are going to be isolated for the next three days in the Olympic Precinct in Homebush, Sydney. While a great part of town, staying across from the stadium means we are without transport and stuck in the sterile business park that the former Olympic site has become. When you know you are not going to play, as is my case, it is usually a bloody uneventful couple of days. The win will consolidate our campaign – a loss will virtually signal its end.

Wednesday, 19 January

T20 Tasmania v NSW

Of all the games played around the country in the last three weeks, this has been the sole thriller to emerge. Chasing 153, NSW flew from the start, making the best of the new ball on a slowish wicket. The spinners, however, were incredible in their defensive skills – mixing their pace, hitting the block hole. The equation quickly blew out from 7 an over to 9s. When Rana skittled the middle order with reverse swing, it looked like an impossible target.

Ben Rohrer then played an incredible cameo, lapping the first ball of the final over for 6 to reduce the equation to 8 off five. A dot, a ridiculous wide ruling and a missed run-out where the wicketkeeper missed the stumps with his gloves heightened the drama. With 4 needed off the last to win, a hittable waist-high full toss was clunked out to square leg for 2 – a win and the good guys go to the top of the table.

Friday, 21 January

I have tried to fit in as much red ball practice as possible during the silly season, often sneaking in before training or at other times when nobody was about. While clearing your front leg to hit to cow can't be good for your four-day batting, the positive mindset of white ball cricket can. All of a sudden I am getting in good positions and stroking it cleanly just by trying to hit the ball. It was a good reminder that intent to score often gets you into the best technical position to defend.

Saturday, 22 January
Club cricket

I am lying on the couch in pain, religiously icing my ankle every ten minutes, having rolled it stepping on an unforeseen ball. I am grumpy and disillusioned as to what this week will bring – I probably caught myself just in time. Perhaps I should think myself lucky. I could be lying in hospital nursing a break. Hmmm. That puts a new complexion on it. My season could have ended today – but it didn't.

I have been relatively injury free for a couple of years now. Five years ago, having broken into the NSW team late in the previous season and with some success, I jumped back to defend a short ball, slipped and in a freak accident, ripped my big toe from my left (back) foot – snapping each and every tendon as well as the joint capsule that holds it in place. That was the end of my season – in October no less. Missing a year of cricket in the competitive environment of the NSW team was the equivalent of professional suicide. I went back to the bottom of the list. A secondary injury to my left foot (tearing 70 per cent of the arch) led to another three months off, and a young gun by the name of Phil Hughes was established by the time I was fit again – in the end, it was these 'black swans' that brought me to Tasmania. No wonder players talk about there being 'cricket gods' when providence seems so random.

Monday, 24 January
T20 Tasmania v SA

Again we showed how far apart our best and worst

performances could be, bundled out for 110 having been suffocated by their spinners. With the winner of this match going straight through to the final and Champions League, it was both embarrassing and horrific to watch. I sat through it in the change room – the worst seat in the house in such situations. You not only watch the train wreck unfold out in the middle, but you see the before and after snapshots as well. I snuck up to watch from the dining room when it all became a bit too much. No need to sit in a losing shed if you don't have to.

They cruised to victory in only the 11th over – one step forward, two steps back. I think this may prompt them into giving me a game on Thursday night if I can prove my fitness.

Wednesday, 26 January

More often than not you know when you are about to be dropped and, more importantly, when you are about to be picked – you can feel the stars almost aligning before the actual selection occurs. Despite not being fully fit – which is often the way in a professional sport full of semi-permanent niggles – it looks as though I will play on Thursday night. I am excited. When you are not playing, you do feel out of it – every tour brings new jokes, every win new memories, every close game a new bond of togetherness through adversity.

My 'manufactured four' options will be the cut and slog over mid-on. As previously mentioned, our analyst's research shows the team who hits the most boundaries (including sixes) will win, regardless of their dot ball count. I don't necessarily agree with this, but have happily bought into the concept and culture that is being propagated. I could hardly have hit the ball cleaner in the nets. I almost wished I hadn't. When you only have four or five sixes in you a season, there is no point wasting them in the nets, is there? Either way, I am sure I will be up for proving a point tomorrow.

Thursday, 27 January

T20 Tasmania vs WA

We had to win tonight to stay alive in this competition, which traditionally brings out the best in our team. We again had a poor start with the bat – which saw me come to the crease late in the third over, but with only 10 on the board. In the last power play over, I cowed the first ball for 4 and then took a risk on the next ball that did not pay off, short cover taking a one-handed catch well above his head that he caught on the second attempt after it had hit his shoulder. In hindsight, I think I got caught up in it all – usually I love taking a single after hitting a boundary just to settle myself and avoid greediness, but I had the captain's message of fearless cricket ringing in my ears. George himself did play without fear, and hit some massive sixes in his 50, while Cossie (having opened) made a well-compiled 40. Strangely, for such a strong player, who can 'go off' and win a game in a session of four-day cricket, he only rarely provides the same sort of impetus in the shorter formats. A hundred and fifty was always going to be too many when we took two early wickets – our defensive squeeze has been second to none. There was a scare, when

Rana twisted his ankle and hobbled off – forcing us to find some overs from our part-timers. Luckily Rhett Lockyear stepped up with his controlled offies and actually ended up our best with the ball. Our inconsistency in the format is baffling, but we are second on the table and set for a preliminary final against NSW.

Tuesday, 1 February

T20 Tasmania vs NSW – Preliminary Final

I have tried to avoid expletives throughout this journal, however to describe tonight's effort as fucking hopeless would be giving us a solid wrap. In a rain-affected game the match was reduced to 17 overs. A few eyebrows were raised when we opted to bat first and the opening balls moved prodigiously off the seam. Again we had a flat start – and again I came to the crease in the third over, this time at 2–6. I cut my first ball hard to point, and then did the same with my second. The third I straight-drove for four. The fourth took my off pole as I tried to repeat the shot. I can't remember the last time I was clean bowled. You feel utterly defeated when you are dismissed like this – perhaps because at its most elementary, cricket is about protecting those three little stumps. At least I can take solace in the knowledge he did not breach my 'defences'.

The aforementioned 'he' was Patrick Cummins, who sent down 147 km/h thunderbolts. Watch this space. Let's pray he is well looked after both on and off the field by the powers that be in the coming years; part of me wants him to be left alone to slowly mature, the other part, knowing bowlers only have a certain number of balls in them, feels that with good workload management, he may as well be thrown in the deep end of international cricket sooner rather than later. There is no need to be wasting good balls on players like me …

At 3–15, the game was virtually lost. Travis and George provided some respectability, but both holed out trying to hit boundaries within balls of each other and we limped to 130. We may then have missed a trick in our search for early wickets by opening with the quicks. Dave Warner went absolutely ballistic – a huge six out of the ground (the biggest I have seen) was followed by 18 off Rana's first over. T20 is good to win. When you lose it is a pretty abject experience – there are no consolations; it is all a mess and a waste. You feel as though you have hardly had a chance to do anything. Maybe I should not feel fussed about playing it regularly. There's a hollowness to it, a lack of scope and possibility.

As you can imagine, our team is a little flat. The party raged on next-door in the visitor's change room until well after we had all gone home. We had missed an incredible opportunity to play in the spotlight of another final. I hope we are not flat with the knowledge of the cash we've missed out on; but I guess just because money does not motivate me personally, it does not mean it does not motivate the next bloke.

Wednesday, 2 February

Virginia, my great friend Tom from Sydney, George Bailey and myself thought of the need to get out of town today and decided to go to Bruny Island. It has become my little escape route down here when things in the cricket world are just getting a bit much. Tom, who had just been released from his role as a contestant in the TV series *Masterchef*, provided great company with his quirkiness and positivity for two downbeat and drained cricketers. Among other things, a few beers in the sun was a great way to drown the reality of what had happened in Hobart the previous evening. We rushed back for Ryan ten Doeschate's unofficial farewell at the pub. Despite his lack of runs, 'Tendo' has been an incredible person to have around the group. His self-deprecation and general attitude, regardless of performance, has been well received. One hell of a bloke, I feel like I have met a kindred spirit. I will be sad to see him go.

Thursday, 3 February

Mark Wagh of Nottinghamshire fame wrote a diary of his 2008 county season. It arrived today in the post. I had no idea it existed until I mentioned this journal to my great friend Paul McMahon, a former Notts player and Oxford Blue, and he suggested I have a read for research purposes. To be honest, I bought it for the intention of comparing notes. Once in my hands, though, I could hardly put it down. I loved it and ended up reading the whole thing in a matter of hours. I admire him undertaking such a project, but also his pure ability to write and think about cricket.

It seems there are so many similarities (thematically and emotionally) that have shone through my diary that also popped up in his, that I hope he does not feel like I am plagiarising parts of his work. An eeriness swept over me when he leapt into a spiel on 'randomness' and Talib's 'black swan', as did his outing of his favourite book of the summer as Rohinton Mistry's *A Fine Balance* – my all-time freezer book (so good I wanted to keep it in the freezer for safekeeping).

Wagh's book should be compulsory reading for all new professionals. We are all human, all suffer from the same fear and anxieties of failure, and are all trying to find the best path to overcome them. My favourite quote:

> The opiate of success is what keeps you coming back for more. There is no better feeling than sitting in a change room after you have won a game, having personally contributed. It gives meaning to all the training, the mental and physical effort. It's the pay-off for risking failure. There are not too many jobs where one's prowess is broadcast to the public on a daily basis. It can be fantastic, it can be hell.

I wish I had written that.

Friday, 4 February

I had an extended hit with Diva today, trying, mainly in vain, to get back into red ball mode. It feels like I am gripping my bat like it is an axe after the T20 circus – holding on with my bottom hand way too hard to be playing with any touch. I am also really flat-footed on the back foot, certainly a product of clearing and plonking my front foot down the wicket for the last two weeks. This flat-footedness is also heightened by my inability to push off my front ankle with any great dynamic force. Such a technical glitch not only limits your stroke play, but also makes you a sitting duck – not forward, not back. In good news, my forward defence has never felt better.

Saturday, 5 February

Today was a great dress rehearsal for this week's coming Shield game, playing club cricket for Glenorchy against Ben Hilfenhaus and Jimmy Faulkner's University. Albeit on a low, slow wicket, I played how I would want to in any first-class fixture – leaving well, content to pick the bowlers off and make them bowl to me. I missed out on my cuts and pulls due to my previously described penchant for leaping onto the front foot with little regard for the length of the ball, but got away with it due to the lack of pace in the wicket. I am sure it will be cured before it really matters, and I am not too stressed – that feeling of going at the bowler with my head is important for my shots down the ground anyway. I would be more worried were I camping on the back foot, unwilling to come forward. I found some rhythm with my routines and generally enjoyed batting in a pressure-less environment, even if my grip on the bat is still Tarzan-like.

Monday, 7 February

Xavier has been ruled out of the World Cup due to injury, despite being cleared to play in ten days' time. It seems very odd considering Australia's first game is not for a fortnight.

Jason has been chosen to replace him. We are now without a spinner on Wednesday night. Jason deserves another crack at international cricket, but I just feel sick in the stomach for X, who has had a career full of highs and lows compressed into two months.

Tuesday, 8 February

I played like a donkey in the nets today. I don't think I was watching the ball – rather ridiculous considering that is the only non-negotiable to decent batting.

The Ryobi Cup Table currently looks like this:

Tasmania: P8, W5, 26 points
Victoria: P8, W5, 26 points
NSW: P8, W5, 25 points
Queensland, SA and WA can't make the final.

Tasmania to play Victoria tomorrow, NSW to play Victoria next week. If Tasmania win one game of the remaining two, we will contest the final.

Wednesday, 9 February

Tasmania 6–258 (Cosgrove 120, Bailey 107, Cowan 1) lost to Victoria 9–259 (Hilfenhaus 4–73)

I am utterly speechless. At no stage did we look like losing – until we did. George and Cossie broke the Tasmanian third-wicket record partnership, both scoring flawless, exquisite one-day hundreds. George was at his absolute best, timing the ball with a full face, Cos preferring to manipulate the pace off the bat and hit the spinners into the stands. We were 2–80 at the break, the Vics 4–60.

The Bailey/Cosgrove partnership then expanded to 226, leaving the visitors needing 8 an over for the last 25 overs. Perhaps this format of the game, for all its oddity, does help create more excitement in the latter half of the game. Although we as players are not huge on the concept, the 'average' Foxtel viewer I have quizzed has loved coming home from work knowing he will see both teams bat and generally end up with a tighter finish.

When the required rate got up over 11 with nine overs to play and only three wickets in hand, I felt we had the game well and truly under control. Even without Xavier or any other recognised spinner, we had remained composed with the ball. Glen Maxwell then played like the proverbial cornered tiger and our bowling went to pieces: from the next 26 balls, Victoria netted 68 runs including the fastest domestic one-day fifty in Australian history. When Maxwell finally holed out, and their final wicket still needed 25 off 18, I think we all assumed the game was dead and buried. In fact, the last two played with ease. George feels we were arrogant, and I have to agree. The coach suggested we are becoming 'gas takers' – a term used for teams who don't like and can't respond to pressure. I think deep down he was seeking a reaction from us but then again, maybe he's right.

I failed to contribute, caught down the leg side off a lifter. I felt like a rabbit in the headlights, not able to ride the rising bounce. I need to fix this pronto or a lean few weeks will follow. We play a first-class fixture in two days' time – again against Victoria.

Thursday, 10 February

I must have hit 200 pull shots today, forcing myself, often uncomfortably, to get up onto my toes and in a position to choose how to play the ball. I usually shy away from heavy volume hitting the day before the game … but I'm now conscious of having said that a few times in this diary, usually when I have done the exact opposite. Funny: maybe there is a stigma attached to people who are so full of panic before a game that they resort to this kind of preparation.

I kept my pads on all session. When I wasn't batting, I was planning and visualising. It has been over six weeks since our last four-day foray. Lots of time to erase the memories of failure and approach the next four games with renewed vigour. Lots of time to lose touch with how to play at first-class level too. I don't feel at my best – I'm just not comfortable at the crease and the bat feels heavy. I am going to pick it up a little earlier and higher tomorrow and attempt to give them nothing. I am still feeling rock-solid in defence, so at least I am a chance. They are coming down with the best attack in the country and will no doubt be disciplined, relentlessly patient and hostile. The wicket looks to be the best of the year, but will still be hard work for the first couple of days.

Sheffield Shield Table:
NSW: P7 W5, 30 points
Tasmania: P6 W3, 20 points

Victoria: P6, W2, 14 points
Queensland: P7, W2, 14 points
WA: P6, W2, 12 points
SA: P6, W1, 6 points

Friday, 11 February

Victoria 233 (Hilfenhaus 4–44, Butterworth 4–62) vs
Tasmania 3–74 (Cowan 25*)

I am exhausted – more so mentally than physically. I have absolutely loved the opening day of this fixture. There is no doubt that this is what gets my blood flowing – there is simply nowhere to hide in four-day cricket. It is the only pure examination of technique, willpower and character and it was so refreshing to be back in the environment of slow, sustained tension. Success builds up over six hours, failure happens in seconds.

We won the toss and bowled in overcast skies (it seems almost every fixture at Bellerive could have opened with that sentence this season). Two early wickets were followed up by some of our worst stuff of the season – feeding their cuts continuously with a stampede of short and wide rubbish. They raced into lunch with no less than 120 on the board – I mentioned to Aaron Finch as we were walking off that the T20 season finished last week, and he smiled wryly. Hilfy was the only bowler who looked as though he knew where they were consistently going.

With an incredible regroup in the middle session we took eight wickets. The wicket looked a little slow and seamy in the morning, but as it quickened up, batting became increasingly hard work – particularly when the lights were turned on and the ball began to swing (something that happens almost instantaneously once they start to take effect). We found our consistency, asked a lot of questions of the batsmen with our length and reaped the rewards. To play forward or back is the single biggest issue of choice when it comes to batting with efficiency. We repeatedly hit an area where it made the question taxing. Two hundred and thirty was perhaps par given the conditions. McDonald and Finch both got past 50, feasting on our first session offerings, but the fact that no one else in the top eight reached double figures shows how difficult it was to get started.

We had 30 overs to bat. The ball swung and seamed. Of course, it always seems to move more when you are batting – 5 degrees of movement feels like right angles. They also gave nothing away, attacking the stumps consistently. No cuts, no pulls; not that I was particularly looking for them given the pace at which James Pattinson and Siddle were bowling.

We could have finished the day well ahead, but lost Dools and the nightwatchman in the last three overs. I love batting with Dools. He has a calm assurance to his game, a valuable commodity batting at first drop. We click on and off the field – particularly understanding each other's cues when batting. I especially love it when he has that look in his eye like he's up for the fight. He had it tonight, but was unluckily undone by some of Damien Wright's nagging swingers. He is laconic and it sadly often gets misunderstood for laziness.

I felt tight, compact, composed. I left the ball with good

judgment – which is a great feeling, because you know you have cost the bowler some energy, while also proving to him you are not going to be sucked in. I would have backed my front defensive shot against any bowler in the world today. My only setback was copping a nasty blow to the index finger on my bottom hand. It feels broken. I can't really move it. It is throbbing like hell and is already black. Funnily enough, though, it solved my problem of gripping my bottom hand too tightly – I couldn't grip at all.

I was bloody proud of my application and intensity at the crease. Walking off after such a session and entering the change room is an odd experience – you are all on the same team, all with a common cause, but are at that moment, at opposite ends of the adrenaline spectrum. They have been half watching and relaxed; you are out of your mind on endorphins, having willed yourself to get through to stumps, and have not yet realised it is time to come down from your high. A sleepless night is no doubt waiting, tossing and turning while dreaming of making a hundred tomorrow.

Saturday, 12 February
Victoria 233 and 2–78 vs Tasmania 266 (Cowan 101)
I did it. Six hours. Two hundred and seventy balls. Ugly as hell. But we are set up to win. There is hardly a better feeling; although I am mainly just relieved. It is a hundred I could not have scored two years ago, which is interesting because the bowlers knew better how to stop me two years ago too. My cut, for example, has traditionally been a productive

stroke. Today I did not get a ball to cut until I was 91. It made me aware just how good the best first-class cricket can be. In this day and age of technology and shared information, I can play a pull shot in Perth that can be analysed by opposition in Melbourne. All Australian domestic games are on a server accessible by everyone. That makes your weaknesses, and also your strengths, hard to hide. In previous eras, the Vics would have known that I was strong on the cut simply through playing against them. It would have been a gut feel. Now they know through hours of footage and statistics what percentage of runs I score through that region. Their gut feel is now a game plan set in stone.

There is certainly a little bit of cat and mouse from season to season, trying to stay one step ahead of the opposition and their plans for you. When I first started out, the bowlers were too quick for me to pull and knew that I was a 'ducker'. Often they would begin and end an over with bouncers knowing that they were going to be dots. After my first season, I had had enough of ducking. I cranked up the bowling machine for hours on end during the off-season – relearning how to pull against pace bowling. Initially it was with tennis balls. I slowly graduated to indoor cricket balls in a move to ensure I did not break my ribs, crack my skull and shatter my confidence. I remember vividly the first game of the next season when Andy Bichel bounced me in his first over and I instinctively clocked him for four over the square leg umpire's head. Bic looked at me in astonishment. 'Where the hell did that come from?' he asked.

Today was a battle every step of the way. I lost track of

time, getting to know every inch of my crease with my continual fidgeting and scratching of my guard. I could visualise the notes in my batting diary as I was doing it:

> Off stump for Siddle – respect bouncer.

> Off and middle for Patto – will try to
> swing one down the line so stay open.

> Leg for Wrighty – nose at the ball. LBW aware!!

> Attack the spinner with a straight bat.
> Hurt him off the back foot.

Mike Brearley used to hum the cello passage from the Razumovsky Quartet as the bowler ran in. Me, I made two taps, took two deep breaths and heard the words of the Kaiser Chiefs' 'Everyday I Love You Less and Less' ringing over and over in my ears (it had been the last song on the team stereo before going out).

Early on, it truly felt like it was only me and the bowler out there, as though he was running down a tunnel at me as I waited. Later, I loved batting with Bails. I cherished those shared moments of intensity that four-day cricket can bring out – the helping, the encouraging and the supporting with even the littlest of gestures.

Every time we developed a noteworthy partnership, they took a wicket. Our lead of 30 could have been 100, but we lost our last four for under 20. I am partly to blame for not going bigger, but my dismissal was largely due to good bowling and not a lack of hunger.

McDonald tore his calf, leaving them a bowler short,

which given their workload this innings may come back to haunt them late on day four. Through the onslaught of bouncers, Bails and I just kept saying, 'let's keep making them come back for another spell, keep getting overs into them, and they will eventually tire'. They didn't today, but will have to at some stage. There is certainly none of that glorious tiredness from prolonged endurance in T20 – another reason I love the challenge of a four-day fixture.

Sunday, 13 February

Victoria 233 and 351 (Maher 3–59, Faulkner 3–66) vs Tasmania 266 and 1–1 needing 319 for victory

I kicked at one in the second-last over of the day – a quicker skidder from around the wicket. It felt like it was missing leg but upon review, the analyst said it was probably hitting. Nevertheless, I am fucking pissed off. Having played so well yesterday and squeezed so much out of myself, physically and mentally – having to turn up tomorrow knowing I will have no bearing on both the run chase and the outcome of the game is beyond tangible frustration. Ahhhh – the highs and lows. I was up for it, just perhaps a little sluggish on my feet after a taxing three days in which I have only been off the field for 15 minutes.

I also dropped a catch – an absolute dolly. It cost us only 40, but certainly the momentum. If I had taken it, they would have been 5 for 100 and close to dead and buried. When fielding at point, more often that not you expect the ball to come quickly. This ballooned and I failed to judge its speed. The moment I expected the ball to arrive off the bat, it didn't, and the panic transferred to my hands – the rest is history.

On a wicket that continues to improve, we bowled well in partnerships for sustained periods. I thought at the start of our innings that we could chase anything up towards 330 to 340. At 1 for 1, however, it will need an incredibly big innings from one of the top five. Sorry, I am absolutely knackered. I feel as though I haven't describe the bowlers' efforts enough, but tonight is not the night. This dutiful diarist is off to bed.

Monday, 14 February – Valentine's Day

This is my first entry of the year written while the game is unfolding in front of me.

1.40 pm: After losing Kruger, Bails and Dools are looking extremely confident and sharp. We have moved to 130 within the first half hour after lunch – 56 overs to get 190 against a tiring attack that is still a man down without McDonald. They are going to have to find a few overs from somewhere, as their two quicks certainly won't have another 25 more overs between them. Oh great. As I write that sentence, Dools had just nicked a cover drive off Siddle. A twist. Anyway, the diary is obviously bad luck. Better put it away.

3 pm: Immersing myself in the journey of the guys battling it out is exhausting me! Bailey is playing superbly. Cossie just hit a full toss down long-on's throat. The diary has done it again. 4–170 with 45 to play.

5.42 pm: Bails has just walked off with 160 not out next

to his name. I just gave him a huge hug. He is drenched with sweat and his eyes are full of jubilation, satisfaction and exhaustion. I am super proud – an incredible innings to win the game with ten overs to play. Jimmy Faulkner played a crucial cameo and we cantered it in as the Vics finally ran out of puff – that's four-day cricket. A mighty win indeed. It will be a roaring rendition of the team song that will be hopefully followed by an old-fashioned lock-in with pizza and a few beers; unlucky for Virginia – Valentine's Day evening will be spent with me in the change room. I'm risking being put in the doghouse for a few days, but it will be worth it. We are now 12 points clear of third, hopefully on a roll and one win in our last three games will mean we are a certain starter in the Shield final.

Wednesday, 16 February

A full day of flying was almost a relief for tired minds and bodies. We will train tomorrow at the WACA, before heading on a bus to Bunbury, a sleepy coastal town three hours south of Perth, taking our total travel time for the most important game of our one-day season to over 12 hours.

Thursday, 17 February

We saw Mike Hussey running at full tilt today, attempting to prove his fitness for the already commenced World Cup. He seems one of the last of a vanishing breed of Australian crick-eters – a hard-working team man born to play Test cricket.

His intensity at the crease is legendary, often freaking out new members of the team with his manner between balls and overs – one recently remarked it was as though he was veteran and nervous debutant rolled into one. For 28-year-old me, he is a symbol of hope and encouragement, having played his first Test at 30. When we crossed paths on the way to the nets today and he said 'Hi Ed' – having never really been formally introduced – I felt a foot taller in the knowledge he knew my name.

Friday, 18 February

Note to self. I need to either start watching the ball in the nets a hell of a lot closer or not go in the nets for the next month. I think, on balance, this far into the season, I need to save what is left of my competitive juices for the middle. Hilfy, with a new ball and close to full pace, hit me flush on the side of the hand – I now can't clench my fist and am writing this scribbling like a three-year-old. I batted like a donkey and fielded even worse. My hand is killing me, so I am putting the pen down.

Saturday, 19 February

WA 6–255 (Hilfenhaus 2–38) beat Tasmania 189
(Faulkner 76) by 66 runs

The equation was simple today – we needed to win to guarantee a place in the final. A spot, given our early season form, that never seemed in doubt. However, such has been the reversal in our fortunes, we are now the most out-of-form side in the competition – incredible given the talent and desire in the room.

Utter disappointment is my greatest emotion at present. We saved our worst game for last. I am a little bewildered at how this second half of our one-day season has panned out. I really am. How a team can run white hot to frozen cold in such a short space of time, with the same core of players leaves me completely dumbfounded.

On an up-and-down country wicket they struggled from 2–15 to 4–60 at the first change. Some took off, some kept low. Most seamed. In reply, Cossie creamed the first ball of the innings to point only to see it caught and I was trapped on the crease to a lowish skidder for a duck – 2–0. It almost felt like a predictable end for me – as though my poor batting in the nets had finally caught up with me. I sat in the change room, a country tin sweatbox, not angry at the result of my innings, but my preparation. Maybe I had been mellowed by the copious amounts of codeine in my system; the carefree dreamy haze had sucked the real anger out of me.

George and Rhett Lockyear steadied and we reached 50 in ten – both in cruise mode as their young and inexperienced attack served up some 'help yourself' buffet bowling. I do enjoy seeing a young quick bowling to George in one-day cricket; the predictability of it all makes me laugh. They invariably try to bounce him, resulting in a nonchalant pull shot to the fence, usually followed up by a nervous over-correction, which usually disappears past him, quicker than it left the bowler's hand. Once the first happens, the second is almost a foregone conclusion. I think the change room just assumed that one of these two would do the job, and relaxed. One wicket was followed by another, and in the blink of an eye we were 6–80.

I watched Marcus North warm up today in the nets and muttered to our 12th man who was throwing me a couple: 'Oh dear, he is getting a hundred today'. He was just so very still. His bat was being swung with surgical precision and minimal effort. He had scored a hundred days earlier and looked a completely different player to the one I had seen both during the Ashes and our previous Shield fixture. He was batting with such conviction. Maybe I was subconsciously trying to jinx him. Needless to say, North got his hundred, putting on a clinic of one-day batting in the latter stages, stroking them to all parts. It felt as though we were playing a game of English League cricket, and he was the pro. No one else looked likely, but we were almost powerless to stop him. By the time he was run out (my first direct hit of the year), the game was out of reach.

We certainly don't deserve to play in the final, but miraculously still can if NSW lose to Victoria on Wednesday night. Regardless, the bottom line is we were not good enough for long enough in this year's one-day competition.

I am off to have an X-ray on my hand. It does not feel broken, but it is still bloody painful to move or apply any pressure. Sadly it is my top hand, and the handle is pushing against the outer palm where it is black and blue. This, coupled with my bottom index finger still not being able to bend, means that simply holding the bat is proving to be hard work. I am trying not to whinge, but caught myself being a little short with a few guys, which is not really my style. Sadly, being impact injuries, Jamo (our physio) won't even be able to work his magic, although he will undoubtedly cheer me up with his ridiculous humour.

If I get some runs this Shield game, they will be among the best I have scored, purely based on the fact the mind is going to have to bluff the body that the pain is non-existent and that a sore hand is not going to affect me watching the ball.

Sunday, 20 February

Conditions at the WACA are how I imagine cricket heaven to be. Generally dry and warm, a fast wicket with even bounce and a lightning-fast outfield. There is still enough open space on the hill to make it feel like a cricket ground, with further heritage value in a rare manual scoreboard.

I made my domestic debut here in a one-day game played on New Year's Day in 2005. On a classic WACA strip, and in front of a full house, Brett Lee was frighteningly quick – a searing bouncer that clipped Adam Voges in the helmet hit the sightscreen on the full. I hit the winning runs in a tight finish. It could have been so very different. With 10 to win, I clunked Brad Hogg down long-on's throat, only to see Darren Wates trip over himself, take the ball on the top of the skull and deflect it for six.

It can be a dangerous place to open the innings, of course, but I have passed 50 in every four-day game I've ever played here. The pace on the ball suits my game, opening up my back foot options of the cut and pull, while making my forward pushes feel like I'm a much better timer of the ball than I really am. You can be expecting to jog through for an easy one and find it racing to the boundary. It is the only ground in the world where I feel like I score quickly. I probably defend and leave just as many balls, but I find boundaries come easily.

It looks like Travis Birt won't play because of a sore wrist, Xavier has pulled up a little stiff with his recurring back troubles, and Butts and Cossie have hamstring strains. I am sure all will make it onto the park, but it is a little disruptive to our preparation to only see half the team running around the day before the game. I, too, trained lightly to spare my hand, but my defence felt solid and purposeful, which I like: too many attacking shots in the nets, I think, fill me with false confidence for the middle. Upon taking my pads off, I told George to pencil me in for at least 100 runs for the game – for a change it didn't feel like I was trying to talk myself into success.

Monday, 21 February

WA 160 vs Tasmania 0–79 (Cowan 29*)

Luke Butterworth demolished WA today with a career-best 6–51. It was McGrath-esque: nipping it both ways at a decent click with ease, abetted by eight crisp catches behind the wicket, including one to me, which felt good after the dolly I dropped in the last game. We were busy making short work of that at stumps, and their decision to play only three quicks seems doomed to backfire: we are going to grind them out of the game, just in case there's a second innings.

Personally, I felt as comfortable and as sharp as I have all season – completely at the top of my game. It seems so easy when you are playing well; you can often forget the effort it takes when you are not. As I was always told as a youngster, 'Enjoy good form, it is a lot more fun than watching'. I was calm, orderly, steady – the way I like to be. Oddly enough, I otherwise prefer my other sporting pursuits to be as free as possible: I aim for heroic passing shots in tennis, bank on miraculous recovery shots to redeem me in golf. But I've succeeded at cricket by keeping it simple, and doing things methodically and fastidiously – it is a talisman.

Tuesday, 22 February

WA 160 vs Tasmania 8–411 (Butterworth 91*, Cosgrove 86, Cowan 81)

The thermometer hit well into the high 30s and the Fremantle doctor took another day of summer vacation, but it was the Warriors who wilted after a century opening partnership, and Cossie's run-a-ball 86.

I love playing in the heat and in a sense miss it a little – Hobart provides little such opportunity. You know the bowlers are suffering that little bit more. It also adds another element of achievement – not only are you battling the opposition but also the elements and your own accelerated fatigue. The beads of sweat dripping down your face and a dry mouth that feels full of cotton wool are a nice reminder that you are working hard and not sitting back in the air-conditioned comfort of the change room. It provides a survival of the fittest mentality, and I love knowing that I have done the work physically to be prepared for such moments. When it was my turn to watch, Luke Butterworth played as well as I have seen him play and his languid cuts and cover drives were Goweresque. He is becoming the all-rounder he threatened to be when he took ten wickets and made a double hundred in a second XI game

Wednesday, 23 February

WA 160 and 137 (Hilfenhaus 3–24, Maher 3–39) lost to Tasmania 426 (Butterworth 99) by an innings and 129 runs

Had I been asked at the start of the season about our chances of lifting the Sheffield Shield, I would have slapped my belly and laughed. Not because of a shortage of ability – it's just that with our dry summers of late, Bellerive Oval has been a hard place to regularly take 20 wickets. Pushing James Faulkner to six and Luke Butterworth to seven to increase our bowling options also seemed to leave us thin in batting. And yet … and yet … We ended the game against WA today in equal first position on the Shield table. Turns out I probably didn't factor in Ben Hilfenhaus' attendance for as much of the season, nor the rapid improvement and fitness of Adam Maher, nor James Faulkner's wicket-taking ability. But really, it's the stuff of mystery: of confidence, momentum, team spirit and belief.

Today again, the bowlers were exceptional: banging brilliant lengths, forcing the batters to play at balls they generally didn't have to, nibbling the ball a little bit off the seam (proving how poorly they had bowled), and most importantly bowling in partnership and suffocating errors out of the opposition. The captain could have asked no more of them. Luke Butterworth is now the competition's leading wicket-taker – one of those quiet achievers who produces wicket-taking 'jaffas' often enough to dislodge good players when they are set.

Adam Maher, our mature-age recruit who possesses a beautiful flowing action reminiscent of Andrew Flintoff, a sharp sense of humour and the ability to hit the wicket hard in the 'avenue of apprehension', has certainly come to grips with the rigours of first-class bowling and now has his wickets at 19 a piece. Mix in Xavier and Hilfy, and we have the bowlers to take 20 wickets at every ground around the country, regardless of conditions.

The only dark moment of the day was Luke's 99. He so very much deserved a hundred, but played this morning like it meant too much to him and he had had little sleep thinking about it overnight. His dismissal produced a collective gasp of disbelief and disappointment. His consolation was being named Man of the Match for his efforts – the third time he has had the honour this season. Most importantly, our cordon is catching everything. Our new 19-year-old keeper Tom Triffitt buoys me – he is a scallywag, but he's got some substance to him. The dressing room is full of belief and trust; the leadership is strong; our one-day blues don't seem to have done any harm. We're peaking at the right time, with three weeks left.

Later ...

NSW and Victoria have just finished an epic battle. Both teams should have won; both teams should have lost. Eventually with 2 needed off the last three balls, the set batsman, 9 down, attempted to pull Dirk Nannes to win the game, but only succeeded in lobbing a return catch.

The result means we have snuck into the one-day final via the back door. Huge screams of jubilation could be heard down each of the hallways in the hotel – as though we were in a pub in Sao Paulo or Rio, and Brazil had just scored in a World Cup final. It's more than a stay of execution; it is a chance for full pardon. In a sense we can't lose – maybe that will be the freedom we need.

From here it is now straight off to Melbourne we go. Virginia is understanding and supportive, but I get the feeling she is a bit lonely at home and the extra five days on the road, on top of the preceding nine, is certainly confining her to 'cricket widow' status. Perhaps we need a dog? I am missing her, and am a little jaded of hotel rooms and bad hotel coffee – but with only three weeks left of the season and the potential of something special in winning two premierships, I keep telling myself a little bit of homesickness can be put on the back burner.

There is rarely any public admission of homesickness – you just get on with it. As a young bloke, turning up to the airport for a trip away with the possibility of a new city to acquaint yourself with was an exciting moment. You could see that it had worn thin on the older team members but you never really understood. For you, it was about leaving a dirty share house and last week's leftovers in the fridge for a clean hotel room and an indulgent dinner allowance; they were leaving wives and kids for yet another week away.

Having now been to all the major cities more times than I care for, I use little adventures, like seeking out new hip eateries, as a method of not thinking of home. I am also fortunate to be able to bring Virginia away on two or three trips a year with me – no longer are tours strictly men's business. When we have been away for too long in her eyes, I try to appease her with the knowledge I could be working 80 hours a week in the city and she would probably only ever see me every second Sunday. She always retorts I would not have a wife if that were my life. It is a trade-off – we are blessed that we get long holidays and days off when no one else does, but consequently, we have to sacrifice any semblance of routine.

Saturday, 26 February

I wiled away the morning hours at a café in Carlton watching the world go by, drinking coffee, writing, reading and was then joined by Gideon for the last few hours, before rushing off to training. Like few men I have met, Gideon could philosophise with university deans, eat pies (vegetarian) with his cricket pals, and discuss fiscal policy with the Prime Minister, making each and every one feel completely at ease in his company.

We trained well today. There was a nice buzz around. For a final, our preparation has been particularly low key. I don't know if it is a tactic from the captain and coach to keep the group relaxed. It suits me; I'm just a little concerned for a few of the younger guys. You don't play in finals every year – it is something to be cherished, not taken for granted. In my first Shield final experience, our captain, Brad Haddin, said something that has stuck with me since: 'People who say the final is just another game is either a liar or has not played in any; they are played at an intensity that can't be otherwise manufactured and big game players relish the additional pressure'.

To take my mind off the job at hand, my great friend Sam took me out to Mama Sita for dinner – a trendy Mexican eatery, where we reminisced about our travel to Mexico City together and the freedoms of our youth. I think we can win tomorrow. I just don't know if the other guys in the room truly believe we can, because of the false pretences under which we've arrived. We shall see.

Sunday, 27 February

Victoria 194 defeated Tasmania 109 (6–70) to be Australian one-day domestic champions

I woke up today with the kind of nerves that make you wish the day was over already and you had a beer in your hand celebrating a glorious win. That sounds like a very strange mentality, I know, but on some days the prospect of what lies ahead can be all too daunting. I consoled myself that I have always enjoyed finals, their additional pressure, and tended to do well in them. I have no idea why – perhaps it is the conclusiveness of the occasion. There is no more to do but compete.

I'm a little dark and disillusioned by the ensuing eight hours. I don't even feel like writing about it, as though to erase the memory without having to relive the pain. Usually the scorecard does not tell the complete story, but today it certainly did.

In a reduced 38-over game, played on a slightly tacky wicket, we cruised to 2–50. In the next ten overs with bat and ball, we lost the game – us 4–19, them 0–50 odd. The Victorians, with wickets in hand, went hard in their second power play in an attempt to bury us. Somehow we managed to claw our way back into the contest – the wicket quickened up and our quicks lifted. We needed 187 to win the Championship.

Even at 6 for 70 at the change of innings, I thought we could still win. I was in, and knew that even if we needed 30 off the last three overs, with two or three wickets in hand, we would be a chance. Dirk Nannes then bowled Butts immediately and we folded. I was 32 not out at the end, but could hardly claim to have played well. When I did hit one out of the middle, it was generally to a fielder. The rest of the time, it felt like I was batting with a pillow – it was one of those days where things just didn't click. It may well have if there was someone else scoring at the other end, as it had in Adelaide all those months ago.

After such a poor performance, there is always that

awkward ten or so minutes of silence. You run through the key moments of the game that went awry and start to wonder what if? Perhaps most importantly, this time also acts as a cooling-off period – a buffer for words that would be crafted with raw passion and generally too many expletives for any significant meaning.

It is almost a clichéd movie experience of witnessing both coach and players in the shadow of defeat. Sometimes you can just tell from the body language of the coach or the captain that a rousing is inevitable – not that they happen as often as one may come to expect. Tonight was no exception. The coach, bitterly disappointed, gave us a post-game burst. Again, the suggestion of our response under pressure was questioned. There was no yelling or ranting, just carefully crafted sentences that were filled with emotion. Perhaps it was more cutting than an old-fashioned, full-volumed baking – the variety that causes eyes to drift to the floor to provide anonymity and avoid singling out. It was an act of a thinking coach, one who knew from experience how to get his message across with maximum effect.

I'll be honest. I had misgivings. Such accusations can become self-fulfilling prophecies – tell someone they are poor when the going gets tough often enough, and they may well just start believing you. But I think he, as we all are, is filthy at how our one-day season panned out from such a promising beginning. He loves this team. He has been a father-figure for some in the room for over 15 years, having coached them as ten-year-olds. He was talking from his heart. It was our turn to listen.

Monday, 28 February

I spent the entire day today booking the Cowans' end-of-season holiday to California. It is as much for me to get away, as to say thank you to Virginia for getting through another season and putting up with me being complexly absorbed in myself. While the benefits of playing cricket in a small town like Hobart are numerous, the downside is that when I am here, I find it hard to escape the cricket world when you live within various golf clubs' distances of several of your teammates – Brendan Drew a chip; Travis Birt a well-struck 3-iron.

It has dawned on me very abruptly that the light on this season is about to dim exceptionally quickly. Three weeks of effort remain. Usually by this time of year, if you are out of the running, the weary body overruns the weary mind and you just want it to end. I am, however, invigorated by the Tigers' situation. The body is aching, yes – my hand is still giving me grief – even doing little day-to-day things like gripping the steering wheel or shaking hands is causing problems. But the mind is telling the aches to quieten down for the remaining 20 days. Where the hell has this season gone? I feel a little bit the same about my career. A split second ago, I was 19 – now I am 28 and a senior player. I used to laugh at the old blokes when they used to say, 'Enjoy it while you can – it will be over before you realise it'. They may now be having the last laugh.

Tuesday, 1 March

Sheffield Shield Table:
Tasmania: 32 pts
NSW: 32 pts
Queensland: 20 pts

I felt completely impenetrable at training today, content to just bat, not looking for bat on ball and happy to leave at will. I joked with the skipper (as I did last week) to pencil me in for some runs. Confidence is an incredible resource. It is wet and cold and there is snow back on top of the mountain. The wicket has 20 mm of live grass on it. We feel that some of the NSW batters, playing so regularly at the SCG, have become flat-track bullies and that we hold a significant advantage in these conditions. Having been on the other side of the change room wall, they will whinge about the weather, the food, the wicket and everything in between. We also spoke in our team meeting that if we can blunt Trent Copeland, their Trojan wicket-taker, the absence of their skipper Stu Clark will mean they'll have to try and find 20 wickets between the other bowlers. Trent has great skill, with his patience, control and seam-hitting ability, but he won't and can't blast you out. Their T20 tyro Cummins is set to make his much anticipated four-day debut and I am personally determined to prove that him sneaking one through my defences two months ago was a fluke. I have no idea if he is impressionable, but it is a good chance to get into his head.

Wednesday, 2 March

NSW 74 (Maher 5–14) v Tasmania 2–204 (Kruger 125*)

I have never been involved in a more dominant day of cricket. Our bowlers were again nothing short of magnificent, on a wicket that played better than it looked. We just did not let up, hardly bowling a poor ball all morning, making them play and, in a couple of instances, drawing out a shot when it was not on. Admittedly, they left the ball poorly, but that is how they play – wanting and willing to dominate. We caught superbly (Bailey in particular) and got on an unstoppable roll; eight wickets in the first session almost defies belief, considering this was a battle of the top two teams in the country. They were missing Katich and Khawaja – but still, 74? Really?

Visiting teams this year have failed to come to grips with Bellerive when there is some moisture in it. First innings scores for the season are, amazingly, as follows: 220 (Qld), 180 (Aus A), 55 (SA), 110 (WA), 240 (Vic), 74 (NSW). Despite being an opening batsman, I would much rather see our wicket producing such scores than 500s and 600s. It can be tricky at times, but it's a fantastic test of character and technique. I feel it is preparing me for tougher challenges ahead. In my career I have done a dust-bowl apprenticeship (SCG) and am now in the midst of a seaming one. I would much rather get fewer tough runs than thousands of easy ones. While my current season average of 31 suggests a lean season, I feel like I have grown as a player.

Last season, I might have fretted that we would somehow find a way to stuff this run chase up, but I have a ton of faith. By stumps we had buried them, Nick Kruger scoring a superb hundred. His addition to the team is providing great stability at the top of the order. It is not just his runs that are counting as his contribution, but his ability to settle the nerves of the batsmen to follow.

We breezed to 40 without loss before I was run out. 'Not involved in another one!' This, though, was one of those that you can't do anything about. Called through for a legitimate quick single, the bowler, attempting to get the ball, cut me off. Forced to run a foreign line, I then had to detour around Kruges, only to see a direct hit leave me 2 metres short. I was on 22 and settled and it felt like it was almost the only possible mode of dismissal.

Their bowling was ill disciplined – but to be fair, they are calling on their last resources, with eight fast bowlers missing through injury (Cameron, Starc, Hazelwood, Cockley, Bracken, Clark) or World Cup duties (Lee and Bollinger). Part of our success has been in keeping our four front-line quicks on the park. In fact, touch wood, we have been devoid of serious injuries all year (excluding Brett Geeves' back). Three of the quicks now make up positions in the top six wicket-takers in the competition, all with averages under 17. The fourth is the Test incumbent, Hilfy.

I think the reasons are three-fold. Firstly, with so much juice in the wicket (not only here but our away games this year as well), only two games have gone into the fourth day (this game feels like it is heading down the same path as well). Three other games have been over by lunch on day three! Accordingly, we bowled less, reducing wear and tear.

Secondly, three of the fast bowlers are over 27 years old. Their bodies have become accustomed to the extraordinary impact on your joints that occurs when the ball is released (over ten times one's body weight in force) and they have already been through the mandatory late-teen back stress fractures, as well as knowing how much bowling is required to maintain peak fitness.

Lastly, we have become the most committed team to recovery in the country. Everyone does it, but to what extent? Alastair Lynch, AFL legend and friend of the team, spoke at our pre-season camp and talked of the 'investment' his three-time premiership Brisbane Lions put into their bodies – including going to the extraordinary length of having their aeroplanes travel at reduced altitude to help soft-tissue injuries. Encouraged by our strength and conditioning coach Sean Murphy, we've pretty much, as a group, given up the booze. Even after a few of our incredible wins, we have been relatively tame, with one eye on the biggest prize of them all – a trophy at season's end. Considering cricket's laissez faire attitude to a few beers after any (or every) day's play in the past, this is a big thing. The results, however, from an injury perspective, speak for themselves.

Every time I have played in a championship winning team, there is a moment in that season where you can pin-point the exact time every single person in the room feels like something special is occurring and you can't see yourself losing the title. Without a hint of arrogance, today was that day.

Thursday, 3 March

NSW 74 and 6–130 vs Tasmania 353 (Kruger 150)

We spluttered in the morning session (so many wickets have fallen this year prior to lunch that I've lost count), but our last four put in valuable contributions to grind NSW out of the game. If they hadn't, the evening session certainly did when we took 6–80. It's a fait accompli we will wrap up a huge win tomorrow. It is hard to envisage a more dominant display. I'm almost praying we 'maintain the rage' as Moey Matthews used to say – our biggest opponent now is complacency.

Friday, 4 March

NSW 74 and 209 (Butterworth 3–33, 3–43) lost to
Tasmania 353 by an innings and 70 runs

It was all over before lunch with little resistance. I found myself drifting in the field this morning, getting way too ahead of myself, and dreaming of wild championship celebrations. Note to self: stay in THIS moment, be in the contest of THIS ball, and the result will look after itself. I have promised myself not to let this happen again as it can be contagious and a distracted team is as good as beaten. A win next week will guarantee a home final.

Tuesday, 8 March

As I write this on our second plane trip of the day from Melbourne to Adelaide, my thoughts have drifted to the perennial Adelaide night one dilemma – a toss up whether to take on the funky eatery, British India (I think the best Indian in the country), or go with the legendary Argentinian steak house, Gauchos, for a perfectly cooked eye fillet and an oversize glass of Barossa Shiraz – first-world problems indeed. By this stage of the season I have stopped looking at what I eat and wondering if it is good for me or how much energy I will extract from it. Touring on and off for the best part of seven months has taken its toll mentally and I am in the mood for enjoying it for what it is worth. We have also booked tickets to a gig at the Adelaide Fringe Festival for Thursday night. I only hope our Friday will be spent in the field.

I am still a little anal with what I do the night before a batting day, I rarely confine myself to the hotel room, for fear of the dreaded thinking time and anxiousness it can expose you to. But too much excitement before bed time, and I feel as though I have compromised my preparation – not as a distraction from the task, but as though I want to put a line through another possible reason for failure the next day, and give myself the best possible chance of success. My career record away from my home ground is particularly weak – only two of my nine hundreds have I made on the road. A statistical anomaly? I don't think so. I often wonder and have previously pointed the finger at the life touring lends itself to (not that I am a drinker or a partier). More simply, I think it is more a question of how comfortable I am in my surroundings at home and that I'm a creature of routine. It is certainly something I will need to figure out if I am going to ever become an international cricketer – their life *is* the road.

Wednesday, 9 March

To the relief of the batters, the Adelaide Oval wicket looks dry and flat. It is not particularly hard, but considering the recent green complexion of the wickets on which we have been playing, hard (and straw-coloured) enough. That last sentence does not guarantee runs though! I am yet to score a first-class fifty at this ground. In my first few games, Shaun Tait used to love my front pad. On one occasion, chasing a miserly 106 for victory, NSW slumped to 6–2 in the face of a Tait onslaught. My first ball was a 150 km/h searing late in-swinging yorker that blew off my front toe. I limped off, using the end of my bat as a walking stick, feeling the blood ooze into my sock. So fearsome was this particular spell, when the 12th man ran out to give Stu Clark a drink, he was heard muttering, 'I don't need this, I have a wife and kids!' If I managed to get through Tait, Dan Cullen would bamboozle me with his off spinners out of the rough. I feel a lot more a complete player against good off spin now, realising it is a hell of a lot easier to play them off the back foot than tentatively prod forward and hope it will hit the middle of the bat.

Again their off spinner – the find of the summer, Nathan Lyon, a fella who was working on the ground staff at season's start – will pose a threat, but I am confident I have the plans to blunt him out of the game. On docile strips, there is always the fear, 'How can I miss out on this?', but half a mistake, and you can find yourself cursing while others pile them on. It has been 20 first-class games since our last four-day fixture here (last season's first and this season's last) and it has occurred to me while writing this, how much we have improved as a group over that time. I, too, feel like I have raised my bar, and kicked on as a player and person.

Thursday, 10 March

SA 6–255 vs Tasmania

Resting Butterworth for the final, our attack looked a little flat on a slow and generally unresponsive track. Perhaps with one eye on next week, none of the quicks hit full tilt. Thankfully Doey, short of a good bowl having come back from injury, bowled with enough consistency, control and guile, to restrict their run scoring.

The SACAs, long our bogey team, did not look like the cellar dwellers that their season had become today, batting in partnerships and generally grinding out a tough day's cricket. There are, though, rumours flying around that the SACA are pushing out their 12-season keeper Graeme Manou. Given he's only 31, we are all in a state of disbelief across the hall in the visitors' sheds. It doesn't seem like a happy place to play cricket.

Friday, 11 March

SA 298 (Maher 3–40, Faulkner 3–59) and 5–61 (Maher 3–23) vs Tasmania 124 (Cosgrove 29, Cowan 24)

We had our worst day today for some time – our bogey team indeed. We were rolled in two sessions. The outfield has been kept long for next week's Rugby Sevens and 300 felt a long way off all day.

I batted for a tad over two hours, solidly and untroubled on a wicket that felt to me as though it was becoming hard to score on, but also hard to get out on once in. I used a new bat. I had felt good with it in the nets but somehow could get nothing from it in the middle. My plan to hurt the offie through the off side off the back foot was sound; his first ball to me was a short, wide one, that I got greedy with and tried to towel to the fence – only for it to turn, bounce and balloon to point off the top edge. Rather than the dismissal itself, I was more disappointed that I got out first ball to a new bowler. That shits me more than anything. Big innings are built around 1 per cent factors such as batting either side of breaks or bowling changes – anything that may disrupt your concentration and rhythm – moments that onlookers take for granted if they are batted through, but are generally times when wickets fall.

As far as dismissals go, mine was soft, but not one that I was so livid with that it deserved a bat throw. That has me thinking – a poor dismissal ratings system based on the length of the throw of the bat? Some of my dismissals this year would have to be well over 3 metres, such has been their dismalness. Not that I am much of bat-thrower. I don't see the point in taking a chunk out of your favourite piece of willow for the sake of anger management. I am a believer in showing your bat some love and it will show some back in the form of runs. I have known players to travel with a bat whose function is to solely bash into things post dismissal – pragmatic I think. I gave the bat its freedom instead. Perhaps Bailey – who fished it out of the bin I put it in – will have more luck with it.

After our poor showing with the bat, our bowlers fired up and dismantled their top order. We sensed that, not used to making the front running, the opposition had no idea how to bury us. They have certainly left the door ajar and we still think we can do something miraculous to win. We can still obtain a home final if we lose, but that would require WA to beat NSW in their concurrent game, and you would not rely on WA to do anything at the moment.

Saturday, 12 March

SA 298 and 198 vs Tasmania 127 and 1–134 (Doolan 78*, Kruger 56*) requiring 238 more for victory

Some days are over before they begin. Such was my duck today. I replayed the shot and the delivery in my head, not wanting to watch the actual footage (how can watching yourself getting out be good for you!). I ask someone sitting in the change room whether it looked as if it swung late (it felt it had after all …). It took me a millisecond to know I should have tried to play straighter, but what did that achieve? The moment of 'doing' was long past. Finally I glimpsed the replay – my visualisation was almost spot on. I tried to clip a ball that pitched on leg and swung away, when a straight bat would have sufficed – caught off the back of the bat at third slip. It was a decent piece of bowling. But there's an end to it. I made a mistake. I need to move on. The last thing I need at this stage of the year is to waste fairly valuable mental energy beating myself up over a minor error in judgment that was made on an instinct – a split-second reaction. I am naturally disappointed not to contribute to the team's struggle, but I don't want to be crippled by the self-doubt of failure. The challenges of next week will differ greatly from those posed by this pop-gun attack.

While it was our bowlers who scraped us back into the game, Dools (who played as well as I have seen him play) and Nick Kruger have given us a shot at an incredible win. Kruges, discarded last season by Queensland, only a game after scoring an impressive 90 against us at Bellerive, came down to Tasmania this season without a contract and no promises of selection. Backing himself to succeed, he has been given a new lease on life. More importantly, he is taking the opportunity with both hands. They both made scoring look easy on a wicket that is getting slower and slower. In Sydney, the Blues still need another 230 with eight wickets remaining. Regardless, I have a deep burning suspicion that we will pull off something remarkable to make the result irrelevant – if we do, we would have chased an extraordinary 170 more than the next highest innings of the game.

Yesterday's rumour about Choc Manou has today been confirmed – a solid reminder to me that your career can be over prematurely and none of us lead an existence that does not have an expiry date – a date that on most occasions is determined by others.

Sunday, 13 March

SA 298 and 198 lost to Tasmania 127 and 6–373 (Doolan 122, Kruger 148, Cosgrove 43*)

Folklore is built on days like today. Doolan and Kruger put on the second-highest second-wicket partnership in Tasmanian cricket history in a chanceless display of batting. Dools, with his pure timing and incredible ability to make it look oh-so-easy, and Kruges, bullying the ball to all parts, complemented each other beautifully – it was a partnership in the true sense and glorious to watch. The wicket turned, but slowly, and such was the complete control and belief in our skills, there were few jittery moments. It was the highest successful fourth-innings chase in over 80 years at the Adelaide Oval.

Our Chairman of Selectors recounted a tale to the group in warm-up of the last time Tasmania chased over 300 in Adelaide. RT Ponting, still then the young punk of the team at 19, told his mates they only needed to get 20 each as he would get 150 of them. Unsurprisingly, his 160 won him the Man of the Match. There was a brief on-ground presentation at the end of the game for Choc Manou's retirement. Rather oddly, to add a further element of sourness to what should have been a cherished moment, Michael Jackson's 'Beat It' bellowed over the ground's PA as he responded to the guard of honour. It seemed to sum up their week.

NSW stormed home to beat WA with little mishap – but it was not enough. A home final has been secured with an incredible seven outright wins in nine games (five in a row), with this win making it a clean sweep of all away fixtures. Despite the lack of personal glory this season is throwing up, I have never been so utterly happy in a cricket change room as I am with this group.

Tuesday, 15 March

It is great to be back home. The last couple of days have been the first time I have realised how tired I really am. Maybe with the light at the end of the tunnel getting brighter, it is harder to bluff the mind that the body is feeling great. My hand and wrist are still killing me, and in desperate need of a rest.

We attended the State Cricket Awards today. Only two of our players made the four-day team of the year (peer voted) – while four made the one-day team, myself included. It is odd we can have three bowlers average 15 and only one makes the team. Brad Hodge pipped me by two votes for the one-day Player of the Competition. It would have brought the game into disrepute if I had won it.

I was so pleased for Mark Cosgrove, now the leading run scorer in the Shield. His selection would have given him great pride and vindicated his move to Hobart. He was willing to take a chance and get out of his comfort zone, and the fresh start is paying huge dividends. I can certainly empathise with his struggles and resurrection. So for that matter can my opening partner, Nick Kruger. We are all interstaters who have had to re-prove our worth, and the ambition to do so has brought out our best.

I had a short but interesting conversation with CA CEO James Sutherland on the current state of domestic cricket after the awards. He was curious as to whether it was good for the development of the game in Australia that so many results were being produced. I suggested, contrary to popular belief, that it was indeed good for the up-and-coming batsmen: the wickets were proving a greater test of technique and skill than playing on 'pancakes'. I tried to make a case that perhaps the goal posts had moved from eras gone by of batsmen justifying Test selection with averages above 60. It was more an issue for bowlers, who were gaining a false sense of achievement and weren't perhaps learning the importance of containment, a skill essential to success at the top level. I also suggested to James, maybe the solution was to produce Test wickets with a bit more life in them.

Wednesday, 16 March – eve of the final

Disappointingly, the National Selection Panel selected a 29-man preliminary Australia A squad to tour Zimbabwe in the winter, and I have been omitted. I found out by reading the press release on the Internet and am now here, on the eve of the biggest 'team' moment of my career, contemplating the realisation that I have individually slid back in the national pecking order. Only three months ago I was in the next best 11 – now I can't even make what feels like a cast of thousands.

The truth is, it is a kick in the teeth – a setback that will have me pondering my long-term future in the game. I am a realist – there is no currency like runs and I may have been short of them of late. But I am keen to know if this spells the end of my dream of playing Test cricket. I have always said as soon as that possibility dissolves, my days in the game are numbered. I have little desire to be 36 and trying to find a real job. Maybe I am just being pessimistic as it is all still quite raw. One thing I do know – I will be using it as an incentive to prove the pricks wrong tomorrow.

Thursday, 17 March – day 1 of the Sheffield Shield final

NSW 5–316 vs Tasmania

My favourite Paul Kelly song is called 'If I Could Start Today Again'. It ran through my head at tea. We had sent the opposition in (correct choice) and chased leather solidly since. I have no idea whether the bowlers were simply looking to ease into the game, or were nervous, or overconfident, or expecting more assistance. Whatever the case, we served up no fewer than 60 boundaries in the first 75 overs to easily have our worst start to a bowling effort for the year. Were the coach's words after the one-day final in Melbourne ringing true? The average first innings score at Bellerive this year is 173, and they have almost doubled this with five wickets still in the hut.

When the ball went soft, the wicket played superbly. The second new ball was then virtually unplayable. It obtained us the wickets of Katich and Hughes, who had been playing superbly, but didn't bode well for us. Privately, I hold a few fears how far back in the game we currently are. It is going to need one of our top five to make a big hundred. At least this is a final, as emotionally exhausting as physically. It feels like every ball has meaning, every second feels like two. Five days is a very long time – so much can happen and we have shown great belief to win from anywhere all season. Someone has taken his turn throughout the season to be the one to win the game for us. That is empowering.

To prove how important last week's win was, it poured today in Sydney, and a ball would not have been bowled. The forecast up there is the same for the remainder of the week. If we do win the Shield, last week's heroics should not be forgotten in a hurry – home ground advantage and not having to win the game are precious commodities when it comes to Shield finals.

Friday, 18 March – day 2

NSW 440 (Doherty 3–67, Faulkner 3–76) vs Tasmania 3–160 (Cowan 80*)

I hardly slept an hour last night. I fear it will be the same again tonight. I'm buzzing with excitement and expectation. At play's end, I'm 80 not out, having batted for four hours, and having come under fire for most of it to aggressive short-pitch bowling from their young tyro Cummins – he has shone like a beacon as a bowler not only of pace but with a talent to move the ball.

Even now every permutation of tomorrow's events are rushing through my head. Can I get 200? Can I bat until tea? Until stumps? What if I get knocked over first ball? From how many behind can we still win? How much time do we have to soak up to absorb a draw? This is endless. It means so much to me, I have completely absorbed myself in our destiny, and I have exhausted myself emotionally because of it.

The day was as closely contested as you could hope for, for

a final. They stuttered and then accelerated; we lost wickets and then recovered, albeit slowly. At 1–7, 440 felt an absolute eternity away. Doolan steadied, and then played a loose shot, Bailey too did the same. My big mate Cossie, now the competition's leading run scorer, was as solid as a rock, curbing his natural instincts of attack and respecting each ball. The more I watch him bat from the other end, the more I am in awe of his prowess. His relaxed nature makes me feel like a worrying mother. Our mid-pitch conversations are hilariously short. He often comes down and just says 'Your turn', and walks off. It has taken me a while to get used to it, but I now love batting with him. He takes the pressure off you with his ability to manipulate the ball with his incredibly soft hands – few hit it later. Despite both being left-handed, we are certainly polar opposites as players – Cosgrove, relaxed, all hands and no feet – Cowan, intense, all feet and no hands.

As for me, my forward defence was tight. I'm yet to hit a ball through covers (maybe finally I am getting the message!), and my mind is willing and determined to contribute. After every innings of substance you tend to get a text from the Chairman of Selectors asking you what your favourite shot was. Usually I reply, 'That straight drive for three', or something to that effect. But my response today was: 'My second forward defence to the young quick – it hit the middle and rolled down the middle of the wicket past him in his follow through. I could see it in his eyes that he didn't think he was going to get me out'. I talked it up a little, but why not? We're still behind, but if Cos and I can bat for at least a session tomorrow, we could well blow this game wide open.

As I write I am washing my 'lucky socks' that I batted in today – maybe I'm going a little bonkers! I've never, ever been superstitious; I ridicule the weirdos who always put their left pad on first. But this week I made sure I had a 'lucky' haircut (the strike rate on these haircuts is phenomenal – four cuts has equalled four hundreds), eaten at my 'lucky' Italian restaurant the night before the game (where I order the same thing every time), had my wife make me a 'lucky' coffee each morning (of the season, that is; I think it is an excuse to not make my own) and am generally carrying on like I'm standing over a craps table in Vegas. I have no idea why! Facetiously, I think it is a bit for show, but why the hell am I washing these socks when there are another ten clean pairs in my locker at the ground?

Saturday, 19 March – day 3

NSW 440 vs Tasmania 6–411 (Cowan 133, Faulkner 71, Butterworth 60*)

We talked as a group before the start of today's play, that if we won all three sessions, beating us in this game would be virtually impossible, barring complete mishap. To only lose three wickets in the entire day was a sign of how far this team has come. They threw absolutely every ounce of energy and aggression at us, and we repelled it like we were the greatest batting team in the world. This was our litmus test. I am filled with pride, not so much with my own effort – that will surely sink in, in a week or so – but more immediately for the two all-rounders who put on over a hundred having been our batting question-mark before the game. Both looked every bit batsmen of the highest quality. It took the big occasion to get the best out of themselves, and that inspires me.

I didn't quite manage the 200 that I had coveted, but I did manage a seven and a half hour vigil, channelling Alastair Cook. Not one of my 337 balls was hit with force through the covers. I kept looking for new challenges to keep myself going – a change of bowler, a change to around the wicket, drinks, repeat, lunch. Sleepless, hyped up on caffeine and Nurofen, starving hungry because I really struggle to eat when I am batting, the innings became a bit of a haze. But I kept talking to myself, pumping myself for the contest – me against the bowler – who would crack first? The rhythm of my tapping and breathing and fidgeting became as soothing as a rocking chair. Minutes became hours, the hours, sessions. I wish I could bottle those sensations.

I did not even watch many replays on the big screen, which are a benefit of the television coverage. Actually, I hate watching myself bat – it 'looks' so much better in my head. What feels majestic is too often shown to be an ugly inside-out bat swing that gives me the shivers. I have probably only watched three or four balls in my season for that reason. While I am aware my mental analysis can stifle me, I'm pretty good at not getting lulled into watching every dismissal in slow motion, nit-picking at technical errors and asking for advice.

My most pregnant moment of the day was in the lunch-room. I bumped into NSW coach Matthew Mott. Motty was a great friend and mentor before he was given the top coaching role in NSW. It was never quite the same after that.

I really struggled to differentiate between 'Motty the friend' and 'Motty the coach'. I think he did too. We have kept in touch, but today felt like it was almost one of those classic gossip magazine 'letter to the editor' moments – the ones where the author bumps into their ex, only for him or her to be a lot sexier than they remember and dating someone a lot cuter than them. We chatted briefly and I walked on down the hall with a Luna Park-size smile.

One thing did become apparent after my dismissal – while not being in control of the team's destiny, I could not watch another delivery that was bowled. Instead, locking myself in the physio room, talking all kinds of things with a wide variety of people. Everyone it seems was the same – busting their guts to contribute on the field but not being able to stomach watching it off. It is a sign of the trust that has grown within the group, but also that we care so deeply for the result to be in our favour.

Sunday, 20 March – day 4

We are still batting ...

I've decided to distract myself this morning by writing. Can this be over already? This emotional ordeal is exhausting to say in the least. There are some jitters about – perhaps as we are so close and we know it. We are indeed further ahead in this game than we are publicly saying to each other.

There are five hours left today – we are seven down and the scores are level. NSW, having to bowl us out again to win, will have to declare tomorrow morning at the latest, but will more than likely have a dip at us tonight. They are up to their 150th over of this innings and are starting to tire. Every over of denial sinks their hopes just a little more.

They will have to come hard with the bat and try and set us between 250 and 260 – not enough on a wicket that is rock hard and has deteriorated very little or played few tricks in the last 24 hours.

Later at Stumps:

NSW 440 and 5–215 (Hilfenhaus 2–32) vs Tasmania 453 and 0–17 requiring another 184 to win the Sheffield Shield

They did not go as hard with the bat as they could have, possibly due to two early wickets, and then set us 203 to win the Sheffield Shield.

With four overs to face until stumps, Kruges nicked his fourth ball to second slip. It went down. I nicked my fifth. It bisected motionless first and second slips. Perhaps they had been blind-sighted by the keeper who had come up to the stumps to stop me batting a foot down the wicket to Trent Copeland. In the end, we picked up 17 runs we don't need tomorrow and I copped some mighty abuse. I have a knack of annoying some players, which I do enjoy hamming up when required, and tonight I did my best to annoy their captain. He was ranting that I was 'weak'; I simply told him not to take it out on me that his team could not catch under pressure. Nothing looks like stopping us now, barring a self-lynching. I'm a little edgy, but confident. It may have been a different story at 2 for none.

Monday, 21 March – day 5

Tasmania wins the Sheffield Shield by 7 wickets (Doolan 68*, Cosgrove 40*)

Very few of us watched much of the day's play again, but this time we were all less on edge and generally more relaxed. At no stage did I ever feel that we were going to lose the game, particularly from 0–50; I could sense that everyone's confidence exponentially grew throughout the day. It felt as though it was a matter of time, provided everyone kept doing their bit when they had the chance, not that that made it any easier to digest. I kept myself distracted, kicking the footy in the nets, willing the game to be done with. With 40 runs to win, and Dools and Cossy cruising, I brought myself out of hibernation to watch the last rites being read. A euphoric sense of achievement began to engulf me. This burning, deep emotional outburst of welling eyes was part relief and part pride.

At 3.16 pm, Mark Cosgrove lifted Stephen O'Keefe to the boundary to seal the Sheffield Shield for Tasmania. We had done it. It was a moment that may well end up as my all-time career highlight. Our team, half made up of players unwanted by their home states and half home-grown talent of an island 1/16th the size of NSW, had just won arguably the most prestigious domestic title in the world. We have become a team that completely, utterly and selflessly plays for each other – doing so with no ego or arrogance. We have all become great mates, a team in every sense. Grown men, many in tears, hugged with the passion of family.

The party raged on, not for hours, but days. Virginia picked me up at the pub at 4 pm on Tuesday. I was still in my whites. At no stage did I get particularly drunk – high on emotion, I wanted to be able to remember every conversation, every shared moment. My fondest memory was perhaps seeing the sunrise over the Southern stand, rum in hand. Those first rays of warmth were a timely reminder of the feeling that filled me up when the winning runs were hit.

My first innings effort with the bat was rewarded with an oversized Man of the Match cheque. The only reason I mention this is that after a beer or two, when I was trying to think of how I would describe such a day to my diary, it felt weirdly like a scene in a movie – a bad movie, actually. But, of course, sometimes even bad movies make you cry.

One other thing:

Sitting here several days later, content and relaxed now that the pressure of the season is over, all I want to do is put down this pen and never to write another diary post again. Perhaps that's another thing I've learned about sport from writing about it: how beautiful it can feel when it is over.

The Australian domestic cricket season

Six Australian state teams (Queensland, NSW, Victoria, Tasmania, South Australia and Western Australia) each compete in three different formats of cricket over the Australian summer months. Those three formats are described below.

The Sheffield Shield – four-day competition

Established in 1892, the Sheffield Shield is perhaps the most coveted domestic cricket trophy in the world. Each first-class game is played over four days, with teams playing each other twice per season (once at home and once away). At the end of the summer, the two top-scoring teams as determined by the points table (with 2 points awarded for a first-innings victory and 6 for an outright victory) compete in the Shield final at the home ground of the team who finished on top of the ladder. The visiting team for the final must win the match outright to win the Sheffield Shield.

To date, NSW holds the record for the most number of titles (45), while Tasmania, only included in the competition for the first time in 1977–78, had their first Sheffield Shield victory in 2006–07. Victoria have won the last two titles (2008–09 and 2009–10).

Tasmania's recent performances are as follows:

2005–06 – 4th
2006–07 – 1st
2007–08 – 4th
2008–09 – 4th
2009–10 – 5th

The Ryobi Cup – one-day competition (formerly the Ford Ranger Cup)

A limited-overs competition was first played during an Australian summer in the 1969–70 season. It has traditionally mirrored the format played in the international arena (50 overs), but has also been a landscape for trialling new and innovative playing conditions. 2010–11 saw the Ryobi Cup played in a split innings, 45-over format for the first time ever, in what was hailed as a bold experiment.

Each team plays each other twice on a home and away basis, usually immediately preceding or succeeding a four-day (Sheffield Shield) fixture against the same opponent.

The top two teams contest a final, with the top-placed team gaining home-ground advantage. In the new format, 1 point is awarded for a 'first innings' lead, while 4 points are gained for an overall victory.

Western Australia have won the title 11 times, while Tasmania has been the dominant force in recent years, having won the competition three times in the last six seasons. Tasmania are the current defending champions.

Tasmania's recent performances are as follows:

2005–06 – 5th
2006–07 – 5th
2007–08 – 1st
2008–09 – 4th
2009–10 – 1st

The Big Bash – 20-over (Twenty20) competition

The first 'Big Bash' was played in 2005 on the back of the growing popularity of the format around the world. Initially classified as 'hit and giggle' – NSW once famously selected Andrew Johns as a publicity stunt – it has become the most financially lucrative of the three competitions, with the top two finalists qualifying for the international Champions League (winning prize money of $2.5 million).

Each state plays only five games in the round robin phase, with the top-placed team gaining a home-final advantage. The second- and third-placed teams play off in a qualifying final in what has been facetiously dubbed 'the biggest game of the year'.

The competition is played over five weeks during the summer holiday period in an attempt to maximise crowd attendance and interest (a record crowd of 43,000 people turned up to the MCG in 2009–10 to watch Victoria play against Tasmania).

Victoria have been far and away the dominant team of the competition, winning four of the last five years. NSW, having won in 2008–09, went on to win the Champions League in India.

Tasmania's recent performances are as follows:

2005–06 – 6th
2006–07 – 2nd
2007–08 – 3rd
2008–09 – 6th
2009–10 – 6th

The PKF Tasmanian Tigers

Coaching staff

Tim Coyle – Head coach
Having played for Tasmania in the early 1990s, Tim has gone on to become easily the state's most successful coach, leading the Tigers to five domestic trophies, including the first ever first-class title in 2006–07.

Ali DeWinter – Assistant coach
A fiery all-rounder for Tasmania in his day, Ali returned to coach in his home state following stints in both Western Australia and Bangladesh. He is considered to be one of the finest bowling coaches in the country.

Michael Di Venuto 'Diva' – Assistant coach
A Tasmanian playing legend and stalwart who represented Australia in the one-day arena, Michael has made the smooth transition from playing to coaching (despite still playing

professionally in the UK during the Australian off-season). He has shared his multitude of batting experience in this role with the Tigers for the last two years.

Players

George Bailey 'Bails', 'GB' – Captain
A devastating middle-order batsman, brilliant fielder and astute captain whose respected leadership saw him captain Australia A in 2010.

Travis Birt
A player of significant experience, his hard hitting has seen him represent Australia in T20 in 2010.

Luke Butterworth 'Butts'
Hobart raised. An all-rounder of great skill and guile. Man of the Match in Tasmania's first Pura Cup victory in 2006–07.

Steven Cazzulino 'Cazza'
Left-handed opening batsman. 2010–11 is Steve's first season as a professional cricketer, having dominated Sydney club cricket for St George over many seasons prior.

Mark Cosgrove 'Cos', 'Cossie'
Having been released by his native South Australia, the ultra-talented top-order batsman looked to greener pastures in Tasmania in season 2010–11. He represented Australia in

one-day internationals in 2006 aged 22.

Gerard Denton 'Dents'

The oldest member of the Tigers squad, debuting for Tasmania in 1994–95. A devastating fast bowler in his prime, injuries forced his contribution to be sadly restricted to limited-over formats last season.

Xavier Doherty 'X', 'Doey'

Left-arm finger spinner who is Tasmania's all-time leading wicket taker in one-day cricket and the state's best and fairest in 2009–10. Still only 27, his best years are still ahead of him.

Alex Doolan 'Dools'

A handsome top-order stroke-maker in first-class cricket, Alex scored his first hundred for Tasmania in 2009–10. Occasional back-up wicketkeeper, following on from his father Bruce, who kept wicket for Tasmania in the 1970s.

Brendan Drew

Raised in Lismore in NSW, Brendan is a fast bowler of immense talent and athletic ability, representing Australia A in the winter of 2010.

James Faulkner 'Jimmy'

Launceston born and son of former Tasmanian all-rounder Peter. One of Australia's soon-to-be stars; his left arm fast-mediums and crisp middle-order batting are developed well beyond his 20 years.

Brett Geeves
Brett's appearances for Tasmania have been significantly limited by injury in the past two seasons. At his best, he is a fast bowler of the highest quality and a more than capable lower order batsman.

Ben Hilfenhaus 'Hilf'
Current Australian fast bowler who is known for his swing and control. His tally of 60 first-class wickets in 2006–07 was the third highest of all time during an Australian domestic summer.

Brady Jones
Back-up wicketkeeper, who debuted in 2009–10 and showed all the qualities of an accomplished gloveman in his first season.

Jason Krejza
Off-spin bowler who made his Test debut in India in 2008, where he took an incredible 12 wickets.

Nick Kruger 'Kruges'
Left-handed opening batsman. Moved to Tasmania from Queensland in 2010–11, where he had played 15 first-class games. In 2005–06 he broke Matthew Hayden's club run-scoring record in Brisbane, but was strangely deprived of opportunities for higher honours in the following years.

Rhett Lockyear
Raised in Mudgee, NSW, but arrived in Tasmania as a teenager in search of opportunity. A destructive one-day and T20 batsman who is also brilliantly dynamic in the field.

Adam Maher 'Mahbo'
Raised in Newcastle, NSW, and late-developing fast bowler. 2009–10 was Adam's first as a professional cricketer, but he has since become an integral member of the squad.

Rana Naveed
Pakistani fast-bowling stalwart who signed for the Tigers as their T20 overseas import.

Tim Paine – Vice captain
Made his Test debut in 2010, having made his one-day international debut the previous winter. A highly talented wicketkeeper–batsman, he is another home-grown Tasmanian to come through the state cricketing ranks.

Ricky Ponting 'Punter'
Arguably Australia's finest cricketer of the modern era. Born in Launceston, his appearances for Tasmania are limited by his international commitments.

Tom Triffit
Raised in the north-west of Tasmania. A young keeper of huge potential who has previously represented Australia at youth level and is a recent graduate of the Cricket Academy.

Jon Wells 'Wellsy'
Right-hand opening batsman. Still only 22, he has shown some promise at the top of the order but is yet to cement his place in the Tigers First XI.